A Spec.

"If you want to go fast, go alone. If you want to go far, go together."
—*African Proverb*

Without question even a modest work like this book, wouldn't be possible without support from those around us. I was able to make my first book happen because of those who came along with me.

Scott Jens – nobody walks the walk like him. His support and drive help fill me up.

Bryan, Jill, Kelsey, Shana and the Madison College Team – generously sharing their resources, time and platform.

Scott Doyle – filling in the cracks in my thoughts, providing additional thinking and helping flesh out the writing.

Steph Spector – polishing the rough stone into a gem.

My Wife Michelle – love, support and "air cover" with the little guy so I could have the luxury of being head down and focused.

The Ships Are Burning

The Ships Are Burning

A No-BS Guide to Organizational Culture, Trust and Workplace Meaning

Scott Kohl

gatekeeper press
Columbus, Ohio

The Ships Are Burning: A No-BS Guide to Organizational Culture, Trust and Workplace Meaning

Published by Gatekeeper Press
2167 Stringtown Rd, Suite 109
Columbus, OH 43123-2989
www.GatekeeperPress.com

Library of Congress Control Number: 2020942491

ISBN (paperback): 9781662902253
eISBN: 9781662902260

People will never go out of business.

—Michael Scott

Contents

Preface

What set this book in motion was a need. A need of mine to articulate a deep sense of disappointment and disillusionment—and sometimes even disgust—with so many of today's workplaces.

Many business owners have seen organizational culture as a nice-to-have. So instead of instituting lasting cultural change, they've made superficial gestures, like offering trendy office snacks, slapping sticky notes on the walls, holding standing meetings, and providing on-site chair massages. Where culture *really* stems from is the very innovation, agility, and creativity that these same business owners tend to stifle in their ranks.

Organizations led by such managers have lost their way. And now we're seeing the razor's edge on which these businesses operate. Part of the reason the gig economy has proliferated is that many people, dissatisfied with self-serving employers, would rather bet on their own destinies than tolerate the assholes and workplace politics and unhealthy norms and conventions permeating more traditional workplace settings. You'd think the one department that has "human" in its name would have the courage to lead the charge toward positive organizational change. But they're always preoccupied with compliance, benefits, performance, and policy enforcement.

What many business owners want right now is for someone to hold up a mirror to their faces and confirm how right they think they are. That cannot be the answer. It's up to us to find a better way to bring about change.

My intention with this book was to provide simple, actionable advice that cuts through the nonsense you tend to hear from culture cheerleaders and false prophets. I'm tired of the usual vacuous suggestions, typically presented like this: *Here's what the research says. Here's what Apple did. Here are some platitudes and obvious conclusions. Here's my sales pitch for my consultancy. Oh, and hire me as your next keynote speaker.* This book most certainly isn't that. What I do share are stories about organizations that horribly messed up with their culture-building activities, and those that have managed to get some decisions right. And while this book isn't a PhD thesis, I also share some academic research in the interest of balancing the more anecdotal sections. Finally, at the conclusion of the book, I share concrete, tactical actions you can take at any level of an organization to begin the process of changing your organizational culture. This book is a praxis, and I present my story to you as a practitioner.

I wanted this book to be useful regardless of whether you decide to purchase any of the culture-building tools that ThirdSpace, the company I cofounded, has developed. If you wish to check those tools out, check the appendix at the back of the book. (There. That's my hard sell.)

I started writing this book prior to the COVID-19 pandemic. But a large portion was written during the early weeks of February and March 2020. As the pandemic worsened, I doubted the book's relevance. Then I reflected on how people were communicating during the pandemic. And then people began protesting for racial justice. That's when I realized that conversations about corporate culture are more relevant now than ever.

People want to feel connected. They need it. They want to matter both in their community and at work. Business owners can't treat their employees as resources or human "capital" then outwardly espouse their support for racial justice; it's disingenuous. And though videoconferencing has served as an effective conduit to help people maintain some semblance of normality in the absence of in-person interactions, "Zoom fatigue" is real; that physical, mental, and emotional exhaustion we feel after a full day of staring at our screens has left many feeling isolated, lonely, and even depressed, seeking connection, community, and new purpose. The glue of culture is going to be critical in the months and years ahead.

As I write this preface, many are pushing for the United States to reopen, and reopen fast. While everyone seems to acknowledge there is a wealth of lessons to be learned from COVID-19, it appears people will be slow to learn them. Here's an example that made me raise my eyebrows: just hours after the Supreme Court in my state of Wisconsin declared the Governor had overreached this authority with his stay-at-home order, people flocked to bars and taverns . . . social distancing be damned. The result was an uptick in cases of COVID-19 infections. We are seeing a similar resurgence across the country after people decided they were done with Covid-19.

Will businesses react the same way? Will there be knee-jerk reactions back to the old modes of operating?

The success of businesses post-pandemic will largely be determined by how quickly they jettison what wasn't working, reimagine work, and implement culture in an entirely new and authentic way that is nimble and forward-looking. COVID-19 and movements for racial equity have exposed weaknesses that have been hiding just beneath the surface for decades. The material in this book is more relevant than ever if you aspire to be a better leader and preside over an organization that is resilient, adaptable, and innovative. It all ends and begins, again, with your culture.

I'm no hard-hitting academic. I'm no stirring corporate guru. But in my almost twenty-five years of experience in the workplace, I've been around dozens and dozens of organizations across industries, sectors, and verticals. I've worked with startups and Fortune 500s. I've worked in factories, and I've been a CEO. The ideas I present in these chapters are deeply colored by what I've lived through, good or ill. I hope my directness cuts through the noise. You and I may not fully agree on everything, but perhaps you'll respect the position I present because I'm willing to take one.

Introduction

The character of a third place is determined most of all by its regular clientele and is marked by a playful mood, which contrasts with people's more serious involvement in other spheres. Though a radically different kind of setting for a home, the third place is remarkably similar to a good home in the psychological comfort and support that it extends . . . They are the heart of a community's social vitality, the grassroots of democracy, but sadly, they constitute a diminishing aspect of the American social landscape.

—Ray Oldenberg

The name of my company, ThirdSpace, was loosely inspired by Ray Oldenberg's idea of a third place: a gathering spot that's distinct from home (your first place) and from work (your second place).

A third place draws on the best of both worlds. Imagine a third place as a water cooler: physically embedded in the workplace, but a safe zone where you can step out of your formal work role, momentarily forget your deadlines, and enjoy the fellowship of coworkers and colleagues. Other discussions of third places reach for other metaphors: the barbershop, the front porch, the lunch counter, the public square, the recreation center. All physical spaces that provide loose structure but allow for serendipity. All providing the comforts of home but also the common ground of community. They often involve a common purpose of sorts, but a purpose that isn't strictly utilitarian or transactional. Connection for its own sake comes first. That's what a third place offers. That's what ThirdSpace as a company is focused on fostering: a sense of connection at work—in the spirit of Oldenberg's third place—using software.

We rub elbows with and bump into one another in third places. When we describe a serendipitous encounter with someone, we say we "ran into" so-and-so. In a post-COVID world, bumping into one another has become a liability, a risk. As a *Financial Times* article on the rise and fall of the office puts it, "The office's greatest virtue—serendipity—is incompatible with social distancing."[1]

During the lockdown, we all spent a lot of time at home, in our first place. Most of us have gone a little stir crazy in the process. We found ourselves yearning for community and connection. We may actually miss the offices we once loved to complain about.

But some of us won't be returning to work. Or we'll be doing so less often. And those second places will be altered, perhaps forever. For the foreseeable future, there will be a lot less bumping into one another.

Where does that leave third places?

---

[1] Mance, Henry. "The Rise and Fall of the Office."

A technical term for remote work is having a "dispersed" or "distributed workforce." Might we also end up moving toward dispersed third places?

There is already a lot of talk about rotating work and school schedules, where we rotate from traditional gathering spots (the office, the classroom) to nontraditional locations (parks, backyards, and porches). And of course, virtual third places—already a growing trend before the pandemic—will assume greater prominence in the years to come. They will serve a purpose, for sure, but they will leave us wanting. We have a baked-in need for physical proximity. The social cues and invisible language that stitch together lasting communities require such proximity.

All of which leaves us with a big question: what's going to hold together this patchwork of dispersed and virtual gathering spots?

In a word: culture. In a post-COVID world, businesses that focus on creating a healthy culture will have more than just a competitive edge. They'll have the key to survival.

So yeah, let's talk about survival.

There's been a lot of discussion about a supposed "new normal." The problem is that normal suggests stability and predictability. The history of humanity (and of the planet and universe) is more often than not one of upheaval. Invasions. Plagues. Ice ages. Meteor showers vanquishing entire species. Stars exploding and wiping out entire solar systems.

Normal is a construction, an excuse to be comfortable and complacent. COVID-19 has exposed normal. It has exposed the fragility of our economy, public institutions, infrastructure, and society. That fragility can't be wished away. We have to brace ourselves for a possible second wave of the virus. Regardless how that plays out, experts warn that for all our progress, we will be more vulnerable to future outbreaks. Our economies and political structures are vulnerable to other contagions.

What is the opposite of fragility? For Nassim Nicholas Taleb, whose specialty is writing about big, unexpected changes he calls "black swans," it's being "antifragile." When most people think of the opposite of fragility, they think of resilience. But resilience is just bouncing back to a previous state. Reverting to the old normal. Nature offers a different model. Nature doesn't just survive disorder and disruption; it thrives off change. Forests that burn down grow back healthier. A broken bone heals stronger at the break. Psychologists now recognize that while in some cases trauma creates PTSD, in other cases it results in post-traumatic growth. "Some things benefit from shocks," Taleb writes. "They thrive and grow when exposed to volatility, randomness, disorder, and stressors and love adventure, risk, and uncertainty."[2]

For businesses, the secret sauce to such resilience, to such antifragility, will be culture. Connection. Shared purpose. Community. Build it and you will prosper. Ignore it and the bursting of the next normal will leave you crashing and burning.

The pandemic has exposed the fragility of our systems, and also their inequities. Going forward, my hope is that managers and business leaders take this moment to reinvent their roles. Netflix forged a new culture by simply trusting

---

[2] Taleb, Nassim Nicholas. *Antifragile: Things That Gain from Disorder.*

employees to be adults. They pruned back the suffocating weeds of bureaucracy and procedure. Sometimes you need a fire to burn away old growth and revitalize a forest. Maybe COVID will be that fire. We now realize how much our lives depend on workers now deemed essential, like grocery store clerks, immigrant, delivery drivers, farmworkers, and workers in meatpacking plants. Will we continue to value and honor their contributions in the years to come? Doing so will require a high degree of civic imagination. How we get there is the topic of another book. But I'd like to argue that the challenge facing business leaders and entrepreneurs is no less steep, and no less a chance at a new beginning. Beyond the profit-and-loss statements, the workplace is a kind of civic institution. It provides people with a livelihood but so much more. It's an opportunity to exercise skills and discover potential. To coordinate around a shared objective. To build something that lasts. To leave a legacy.

I hope this book leaves behind its own modest legacy: a few breadcrumbs to help you chart a path through the uncertainty that lies ahead. Be bold. Pay attention to the little things. Don't settle for the false security of normal.

The pandemic and the protests have humbled me by showing me how much of the world I don't understand. But it has also shown me how much more there is to discover. I have glimpsed with new clarity how fragile are our structures and our fictions, and how precious. How next time, we might rebuild them, stronger.

The ships are burning in the harbor, and there is only one way. Up the hills to explore and build.

CHAPTER 1

What Is Culture? And Why Is It Important?

If we are to achieve a richer culture, rich in contrasting values, we must recognize the whole gamut of human potentialities, and so weave a less arbitrary social fabric, one in which each diverse human gift will find a fitting place.

—Margaret Mead

Culture is a thousand things, a thousand times. It's living the core values when you hire; when you write an email; when you are working on a project; when you are walking in the hall.

—Brian Chesky

Numerous leaders acknowledge that it's the heart of employee engagement, innovation, and agility—but culture is still an elusive topic in the business world. Like Schrodinger's cat, we try to sneak up on it—label it, classify it—but it eludes us in practical implementation. Culture's got at least nine lives.

Or, in the *American Heritage Dictionary of the English Language*, eight definitions as a noun alone. "Intellectual and artistic activity." "A colony of bacteria." (As in a cup of yogurt.) "The totality of socially transmitted behavior patterns, arts, beliefs, institutions, and all other products of human work and thought." (Wow, that's a mouthful.) I'll stop there.

Yet culture started off as a pretty simple and elemental activity: namely, the tending of a living thing, mainly crops or animals. Later in human history, it evolved into something more abstract: the tending of human development, and the results of that process.

At ThirdSpace, we aim to demystify the idea of culture and take it back to its roots. We like to think of culture as a simple human process founded on first principles, rather than an abstract and elusive byproduct. Culture is something that's alive and evolving, not something gathering dust on a company mission statement. Culture is what happens at the water cooler. Culture is a conversation, starting with a connection among people.

If culture has a long history as a word, it has a longer history as an activity. Human beings became anatomically and biologically modern (that is, in our current form as *homo sapiens*) about 200,000 years ago. But we didn't become behaviorally modern until about 50,000 years ago. That's when we started developing language, abstract thinking, symbolic expression—and the shared norms and values of human culture.

At that same time, humans started forming more fixed groups or tribes. The glue that held these groups together was a shared ethos of cooperation, and eventually of empathy. This aspect of human evolution puzzled Darwin so much he called it the paradox of altruism.[3] How could the process of natural selection, driven by the self-interested dynamic of survival of the fittest, produce such unselfish behavior and impulses? It turns out that survival of the fittest at the individual level and at the group level are two different things. Our survival and self-interest as a group required us to act beyond our self-interest as individuals.

This, really, is the essence of culture—whether for an ancient hunter-gatherer tribe or a modern Silicon Valley startup team. We form a group that becomes more than the sum of its parts. That allows us members to transcend individual self-interest and achieve something more than we could on our own.

Trust

What hunter-gatherer tribes were cultivating among one another was, in a word, trust. Trust in the business world has been the focus of Harvard Business School professor Amy Edmondson for almost thirty years. In 1991, while studying organizational behavior at Harvard, Edmondson started researching error rates at various units in Boston-area hospitals. There, she found her own paradox: teams that reported the most errors weren't actually the most error-prone. They were the ones where team members felt the most comfortable *talking* about their mistakes. So in fact these were the best teams, where employees could talk about mistakes (their own, and those they observed) openly and

---

[3] Lehrer, Jonah. "The Paradox of Altruism."

without fear of reprisal or punishment. And if they could talk about those mistakes, they could learn from them and get better. Edmondson coined the term "psychological safety" to describe the set of unwritten rules that enabled members of a team to be their authentic selves, speak up, and take risks.[4]

As Mister Rogers used say, "Anything mentionable is manageable."

Google came across Edmondson's research in 2012, when they launched Project Aristotle, an internal inquiry into why certain teams at Google were more productive and innovative than others. They found no correlation between a team's composition and how well it performed. "The *who* part of the equation didn't seem to matter," said one executive. It was the *how*—the group's shared social norms, the trust it engendered. Productivity and innovation depended on a team's culture.

Google is a company built on Big Data. That's their business model. So when they conclude that traditional business metrics can't capture what makes for great team and organizational culture, we should all sit up and take notice. They realized what Leandro Herrero of the Chalfont Project has been preaching for years. "I want leaders to be experts in small data," said Herrero. "The seeing and feeling, the perceptions and insights, the said and above all unsaid."[5] Soul sucking goal setting sessions, annual employee reviews,

---

[4] Edmondson, Amy. "Psychological Safety and Learning Behavior in Work Teams."

[5] Duhigg, Charles. "What Google Learned from Its Quest to Build the Perfect Team."

OKRs, 360-degree feedback, whatever your soup de jour, it doesn't build trust much less your culture.

The Cost of Ignoring Culture

Unfortunately, too many business leaders at best give lip service to culture. Talking about her book *The Fearless Organization*, Edmondson says that shared trust and psychological safety in teams remain the exception, not the norm. Companies are still narrowly focused on traditional metrics. Doing so may make a business leader appear "hard-nosed," she says. "But it's also out of touch with reality."[6]

A 2020 report on culture by Accenture underscores just how out of touch many executives are:

- While 68% of leaders feel they are creating an empowering work environment, only 36% of employees agree.
- 76% of leaders believe their employees have good control over when, where, and how they work; only 29% of employees agree.
- Leaders estimate that employees who do not feel "included" constitute only 2% of the workforce; in fact, 20% feel this way.

Surveying over 1,700 executives in 28 countries, the report found that only 21% of leaders designate company culture as a top priority. Asked why, the executives cite how difficult culture is to measure and how inconclusive the link

---

6 Nickisch, Curt. "Creating Psychological Safety in the Workplace."

between culture and business results is.[7] These lazy excuses reveal how often leaders look only at the short-term horizon and quarterly balance sheets. The link is inconclusive only if you're looking in the wrong places. Google looked in the right places—at the nuances of human behavior that business metrics can't measure—and found a clear connection between culture and performance. Some might say, "Well, Google can afford to spend resources on culture." But that's beside the point. Yes, Google spent time and money studying what makes a great team. But in the end, they discovered that the secret sauce to great teams is decidedly low-tech and low-cost. A lack of financial resources isn't a reasonable excuse not to act within your organization.

Ignoring culture comes at a high price. Gallup's research finds that just three in ten U.S. employees strongly agree that their opinions seem to count.[8] If you doubled that ratio to six in ten, organizations could realize a 27% reduction in turnover, a 40% reduction in safety incidents, and a 12% increase in productivity.

What do you get when employees don't feel like their opinion counts? You get Wells Fargo. Strong top-down pressure to meet ambitious sales targets led the company down a slippery slope of questionable business practices that no one felt comfortable speaking up against. The result was a massive scandal and a $185 million fine.

---

[7]   Accenture. "Getting to Equal: The Hidden Value of Culture Makers."
[8]   Dvorak, Kate and Pendell, Ryan. "Want to Change Your Culture? Listen to Your Best People."

Wells Fargo's story illustrates not just the cost of failing to build a good culture, but the cost of denying an unhealthy culture. The executives at the top never took responsibility for the rotten culture they had built. Even when Wells Fargo let go of 5,300 employees, its top executives blamed the scandal on "bad apple" employees. They didn't point to the company policies and practices that encouraged aggressive "cross-selling"—pushing customers who had already purchased one of the company's product lines to buy another. Cross-selling was, according an expert interviewed by *The Wall Street Journal*, a "religion" at Wells Fargo. That was their culture.[9]

The Path to Great Culture: Thinking Small, and Thinking Big

Creating great organizational culture is hard, ongoing work, but it's not rocket science. Return to the idea of culture as tending the soil. Where leaders cultivate an environment that encourages authenticity, candor, risk-taking, and empowerment, great culture will grow.

Don't get bogged down in a rear-view mirror metric like employee engagement. Pay attention to small data, that is to say the "micro-tells" of the organization, to forward-looking information that gives you a sense of what's going on around the water cooler. Identify what sows the seeds of trust—the glue that makes teams and organizations cohesive, and that enables them to become more than the sum of their parts.

---

[9] Glazer, Emily and Rexrode, Christina. "Wells Fargo CEO Defends Culture, Lays Blame with Bad Employees."

Culture lives in the minutiae, in the small details, in the "thousand things" Brian Chesky refers to in the quote that opens this chapter. *We are what we repeatedly do,* goes a saying widely (and wrongly) attributed to Aristotle. But it captures perfectly one of the themes of this book, and a central tenet of Third Space. Culture is behavior, not pronouncements.

Culture also lives in the big picture, in what we like to call *awe.* Awe may seem far larger and grander than trust, the other emotion we've highlighted in this chapter. Yet awe and trust are companion sentiments. Both are about being a part of something greater than ourselves. Two primary features of awe are 1) a diminished ego, and 2) an increased sense of connectedness to others. These are the same qualities that allowed hunter-gatherers to put the good of the group over the self-interest of individuals.

What does this have to do with organizational culture? A company's mission, if it truly expresses lived values embodied in how employees go about their business, can elicit its own kind of awe. Authentic vision can turn mission into a shared North Star.

You can mine awe in any business. Here's an excellent example, from the complete text of Apple's iconic "Think Different" ad:

> *Here's to the crazy ones.*
> *The misfits.*
> *The rebels.*
> *The troublemakers.*
> *The round pegs in the square holes.*
> *The ones who see things differently.*

They're not fond of rules.
And they have no respect for the status quo.
You can quote them, disagree with them, glorify or
vilify them.
About the only thing you can't do is ignore them.
Because they change things.
They push the human race forward.
While some may see them as the crazy ones, we see genius.
Because the people who are crazy enough to think
they can change the world, are the ones who do.

When you hear the ad narrated by actor Richard Dreyfus, over a black-and-white reel of historical figures like Albert Einstein, Bob Dylan, and Martin Luther King, it's hard not to feel chills run down your spine. And yes, a sense of awe.

You might counter by saying: my business is selling tires— where's the awe in that?

It's all in how you frame it. Think about entrusting your life, and that of your family, with 150 square inches of rubber and steel standing between your car and the highway. That's how Michelin framed it when the company crafted its simple motto:

Because so much is riding on your tires.

Yale School of Management professor Amy Wrzesniewski has studied this reframing at the individual level. She calls it "job crafting." And that's not just clever spin to chocolate-coat the broccoli. In one of her first studies, she interviewed custodial staff at a hospital. What she found was a group of highly motivated employees who didn't see themselves as simply janitors. They framed their humble daily task in terms of a higher mission: creating a safe and clean space in which patients could get better. They saw themselves as healers.[10]

With this attitude shift, they transformed a job into a calling. These workers did it on their own. Think of what job crafting could accomplish if it were a collaboration between business leaders and their employees. If, instead of just slapping a new label on an existing job, a manager coached their employees to reconfigure their jobs in a way that maximized their personal and professional development. That's the transformative power of culture in action. This creates a sense of autonomy for employees, which is a pillar of self-determination theory. I'll discuss this further in later chapters.

By itself, a task is just a task. Tethered to a mission, a vision, a North Star, it's another thing entirely. As Antoine de Saint-Exupéry, the famed author of *The Little Prince,* put it:

> *If you want to build a ship, don't drum up people together to collect wood. Don't assign them tasks and work, but rather teach them to long for the endless immensity of the sea.*

---

[10] Zax, David. "Want to be Happier at Work? Learn How from These Job Crafters."

CHAPTER 2

Cultivating Connection: How Do You Seed Culture?

The best way to find out if you can trust somebody is to trust them.

—Ernest Hemingway

That trust is built in drops and lost in buckets.

—Kevin Plank

In 2014, researchers at Stanford compared two groups of volunteers who were assigned to solve a challenging puzzle. Both groups went through the same routine. First, they met briefly as a group. Then they were sent to separate rooms to work on a puzzle. As they worked, both groups received a tip that would help them complete the puzzle.

The first group was told they were working on the puzzle as individuals; there was no mention of their working together in any way. The tip they received later was, they were told, from one of the researchers. This was dubbed the "psychologically separate" group.

The second group was told they were working on the puzzle together—even though, just as the other group, they were each working separately in their own room. Later, they received the exact same tip as the first group but were told it came from a fellow participant. This was dubbed the "psychologically together" group.

The experiment was conducted multiple times, each with the same result. The members of the "psychologically together" groups performed better, reported more interest, and persisted 48%–64% longer.

Though seemingly inconsequential, the social cues that the "psychologically together" groups received had major ripple effects. They produced a significant uptick in focus and engagement.[11]

Imagine the sustained effect of making cues of belonging an integral part of your organizational culture.

Social Cues

Culture can sound like an elusive, intangible, vague, and ethereal ideal, especially to hardcore business types. (A corporate venture capitalist once told me he wasn't interested in culture because it was too "squishy." It was especially confounding because his parent firm sells employee benefits.) But it doesn't have to be that way. Culture is not squishy.

Daniel Coyle, author of *The Culture Code*, specialized in researching highly successful teams. He believes that the DNA of a healthy culture is made up of trust, safety, vulnerability.

---

[11] Parker, Clifton. "Stanford research shows that working together boosts motivation."

In studying successfully teams, he noticed "a distinct pattern of interaction" that was "located not in the big things but in little moments of social connection." In other words, their success was rooted in action.

What people *do* engenders trust, safety, and vulnerability. And in turn, that creates a healthy culture.

The MIT Human Dynamics Lab is trying to identify and measure the subtle behaviors—the social cues, or as anthropologists call them, forms of human signaling—that contribute to creating group safety and trust. "Modern society is an incredibly recent phenomenon," says Sandy Pentland, who runs the lab. "For hundreds of thousands of years, we needed ways to develop cohesion because we depended so much on each other. We used signals long before we used language, and our unconscious brains are incredibly attuned to certain types of behaviors."[12]

MIT's research shows that great teams display definite patterns of interaction. In such teams, everybody talks and listens in roughly equal measure. Contributions are short. There is no grandstanding. Team members communicate directly with one another, not just to leadership. Members carry on side conversations within their team. They also engage others outside of the team and report that information back to the group.[13] (As a cautionary note, be aware that "reporting" can create a friction, overhead, and feeling of surveillance. Bringing value back to the group should offer

---

[12] Coyle, Daniel. *The Culture Code: The Secrets of Highly Successful Groups.*
[13] Pentland, Alex. "The New Science of Building Great Teams."

the "reporters" a sense of accomplishment and excitement because their discovery has increased the value of the entire group.) While MIT's researchers found that some meetings were more effective than others, they concluded that informal interactions were the most powerful. "The best predictors of productivity," Pentland writes, "were a team's energy and engagement outside of formal meetings."

These patterns are nearly identical to those that Google found in their highest performing teams. While both Google and MIT have attempted to quantify this behavior, that's not necessary for most astute and empathetic leaders, who should be able to read the room and assess how well their own teams conform to these qualities.

Social cues really all boil down to a simple message: *you are safe here.*

You can build these cues into your culture by design. For instance, my ThirdSpace co-founder Dr. Scott Jens and I built our partnership as a spin-off of my previous startup, Ronin Studios. SJ was busy building his own startup at the time—Rev360—which was on *Inc.* magazine's list of fastest-growing companies. So he entrusted me with handling a growing stack of expenses and logistics that all software startups have to power through.

There were times where I didn't have a chance to connect with SJ for weeks. I would sometimes pay for our expenses on a credit card. I'd send SJ legal docs to be signed, and he'd sign them. No lawyering up. No quibbling over details. He trusted me to take the lead on essential work. And even though I made my share of mistakes, his trust in me never wavered. At a gut level, I knew he had my back. That display of faith allowed me to grow as a person, entrepreneur, and business leader in ways that my MBA program never made possible for me.

In countless ways, spoken and unspoken, SJ signaled his trust in me.

Similarly, in ThirdSpace's culture-building software, we've integrated very subtle cuing to prime behavior. Users of ThirdSpace have seen powerful results grow out of simple choices: selecting certain iconography, visuals, word choices, and colors for their "spaces," which serve as a kind of message board. The ability to invite somebody into a "space," too, demonstrates an extension of trust.

Build a Culture of Commitment

In the 1990s, James Baron and Michael Hannan of the Stanford Project on Emerging Companies analyzed the founding cultures of 167 Silicon Valley startups. They identified three basic models for creating positive cultures:

1. The Professional Model – Build and adhere to policies, procedures, and rules that follow a hierarchical structure.
2. The Star Model – Recruit and hire the best talent.
3. The Commitment Model – Develop a group with shared values and strong emotional bonds.

The Professional Model, while it worked in some cases in the late 20th century, was largely found to be full of shortcomings. The Star Model produced better results. But it wasn't as effective as the Commitment Model. Where the latter stood out was in the area of resilience. Despite the bursting of the dot-com bubble, none of the Commitment Model companies failed. Moreover, they succeeded in achieving IPOs three times more often.

One tactic backfired in the Commitment Model, though. In "Commitment Counts," a summary of the research published in MIT's business journal, the researchers "found evidence suggesting that companies may be penalized for espousing commitment values without backing them up."[14] So if you're going to follow the Commitment Model, you better, well, commit to it.

I've been part of companies where management appeared to commit to real cultural change, only to later undermine their own cause through caustic, divisive behavior. While I was working at a large F500, I saw the formation of a team that was supposed to focus on innovation. The team's mission was ill-defined, and the result was this Star-Bellied-Sneetch feeling from the rest of the organization. However, the director in charge of this team felt that having Macs instead of ThinkPads, constant showboating, cool snacks, and special workspaces symbolized that this team was capable of creating lasting change.

It was a superficial veneer. The team struggled with actual innovation and integrating their work back into the eighty-year-old organization. When the director was confronted with the cultural shift needed to produce the required innovation results, he and other leaders took that as a challenge to authority. They would target dissenters, install members of the

---

14 Kwak, Mary. "Commitment Counts."

team as spies to report on others who weren't towing the party line, fabricate lies, and terminate those who didn't comply. The replacements were buddies and fraternity brothers. This team lacked trust and worked out of fear, and the director was just a bureaucrat looking for a bump up the org chart. If that leader had been honest about their ambition with themselves and others, the team could have worked around that. A team that was supposed to be the tip of the innovation spear for corporate innovation operated in fear and frustration. It had financial support but lacked (and craved) leadership that was humanistic, authentic, and genuine.

Again, it's about behavior—*repeated* behavior—and not pronouncements, executive offsites, speeches, a lofty mission statement, or any of the other trappings and window dressings I've referred to as "culture theater." There are no shortcuts or hacks that can fast-track you to a culture of commitment and connection. You must build it: slowly, methodically, patiently, humbly.

One such repeated behavior that leaders can implement themselves and model for the rest of the company is authenticity. You can't be authentic unless you're willing to be vulnerable. Willing to be yourself, unapologetically, minus the mask and the pose and bravado. It's no accident that 85% of the "changemakers" we talked about believe that leaders should be the same person on the job as they are off the job. Leaders who act out this belief also extend that same freedom to their employees. When employees feel free to bring their whole selves to work, risk-taking and the innovation that comes with it increase exponentially. Cynical old guard bristle at this suggestion because they don't want people bringing their personal problems to work. Guess what? They have always done so and will continue to do so anyway. Furthermore, how do you expect someone to shut part of themselves off for nine to twelve hours and pretend? You can't. Organizations that expect employees to be able to switch off emotionally aren't being realistic.

We tend to think of trust as a foundation. The solid ground that allows us to be vulnerable. But it works the other way. Vulnerability precedes and enables trust.

These are some of the most powerful words a leader can utter:

> *I don't know.*
> *I'm scared.*
> *I need your help.*
> *What do you think?*
> *I screwed up.*
> *I'm stuck.*
> *I'm unsure.*
> *I'm lost.*

At many companies, unfortunately, the leadership talks trust and culture—but they put in place a bramble of rules and procedures that signal the opposite. This creates relationships that are less like the partnership SJ and I had formed, and more like your relationship with your auto mechanic. Before you let them touch the car, you get an estimate. You sign off on a detailed list of work to be done. You place a not-to-exceed limit on the work. You may shake hands (although watch out for the monkey wrench behind his back), but fundamentally, there isn't an overwhelming feeling of trust in the process.

When cues of belonging and connection—and vulnerability and trust—become part of a larger culture and are absorbed into your organization's DNA, you move from *I am safe here* to *We are safe and connected here.*

CHAPTER 3

How Do You Sustain Culture? (And Why So Many Companies Fail)

Show me a preacher who has lost their spirit, and I'll show you someone who never had it to begin with.

—Unknown

One of the reasons my partner Dr. Scott Jens and I started ThirdSpace was that I could see so many companies trying to get culture right and falling short.

In some cases, executives gave lip service to culture without fully committing to it. But in many cases, leadership sincerely tried to create a healthy culture because they knew it was important. Still, they weren't getting it right.

Some early-stage companies I worked with burst out of the gates with a committed core team led by a charismatic founder. After weathering early struggles, like every startup must, they'd create a breakthrough product and explode onto the scene. But that early momentum didn't always have staying power. As the organization grew and changed, they lacked the energy to sustain their culture.

Seeding culture, as we've explored in the first two chapters, is one thing. Creating a lasting culture that will stand the test of time is quite another.

Growing Pains

In their first years, many companies are fueled by the charisma, personal vision, and sheer willpower of their founder. Provided the founder surrounds themselves with a loyal crew willing to ride the inevitable ups and downs, their force of personality can stand in for real company culture . . . for a while. At this point, the company may be said to have more of an attitude than a real culture. There may be a certain camaraderie among the founding team as well—but will that translate into the future as the company grows and takes on new employees?

For years, the standard pattern was that a company's financial backers would decide at some point that the founder, however original or creative they might be, lacked the discipline to steer the company to sustained profitability. Steve Jobs getting fired by Apple is a prominent example.

Even when the founder sticks around, those growing pains are real. When I founded Ronin Studios, I had to juggle dealing with the operations of a growing business, building creative, game-based learning products, and trying to create culture with employees who were working for equity and below-market wages. At our largest headcount, we had eleven full-time employees. Every day, each of them had the power to put wind in our sails or pull us down. I'd do my best to pump up the team, share the good, bad, and ugly, but there so many days when I felt woefully inadequate for that role of chief culture officer. It was a challenging to shift gears throughout the day: one moment dealing with spreadsheets, software bugs, angry customers, or potential investors, and then having to rally the team. It felt like failure to admit that I, as the keeper of the organization's vision, may not have the long-term energy to help the talent weather the ups and downs.

Yet it didn't feel right to find a surrogate, either. As a leader, I felt stuck. So I can understand the desire to use extrinsic rewards as proxy for emotional leadership. Emotional leadership is exhausting, and filling the team up is a daily necessity! You don't put friendship, love, trust, and connection on a calendar for thirty minutes each week. A problem with extrinsic motivation is that when the money gets tight and you can no longer provide those incentives, then you're left with a shell.

I eventually closed Ronin because of a confluence of several factors. Coming to grips with the experiment that it was has helped me to reflect and learn. It was one of the toughest, scariest things I've ever undertaken. I never told my Ronin team that.

Replacing a founder with a suit may bring a degree of polish and professionalism, but at what cost? As we saw in the last chapter, startups that tried to "professionalize" their culture and replace personal commitment with procedure didn't fare well under the pressure of the 2008 financial crisis. And Apple certainly lost some of its edge and soul, paving the way for Steve Jobs's eventual triumphant return.

In more recent years, founders have figured out a way to legally insulate themselves from being dislodged with tight founder agreements. But that carries its own set of problems. When a company's culture rests almost entirely on the personality of its founder, that can lead to toxic cultures that implode in scandal. Exhibit A: the "bro culture" of founder Travis Kalanick that brought Uber a wave of sexual harassment lawsuits.

No, a fulfilling culture doesn't just happen on its own. It's something you must inculcate deliberately and thoughtfully—and sooner rather than later.

New Blood

For a startup beginning as a group of tightly knit friends, expanding beyond that core group is another kind of growing pain. Here you face a new challenge: moving from a culture that may have taken shape organically and been largely implicit, to one where that culture must be made explicit to newcomers, and thus thought about in a more conscious, deliberate way.

The communication of culture should not be a one-way street. New hires are not just there to fulfill a task and to assimilate into your culture as in the Star Model. As we talked about in the last chapter, you get the most out of employees when you encourage them to bring their whole selves to work. A new employee brings a unique set of experiences and a unique point of view; they will add to and change both the group dynamic and the culture, however subtly. That can be a good thing.

Far too often, however, "onboarding" (as we have come to call it in HR-speak) is a sterile operational process and a one-way conversation. On day one, you fill out the paperwork. You are shown the bathrooms, given a spin around the facility, shown your work area, and then left there for the next week until someone figures out what to do with you. Oh, you're also given the soul-sucking task of studying the corporate intranet.

This may sound like a horrible joke, but unfortunately, it's a kind depiction . . . and all too common. Some organizations even refer to this as induction. Unless it's into the Rock and Roll Hall of Fame, who the hell wants to be *inducted*.

What's wrong with simply welcoming someone into your organization? See that first day as kicking off an ongoing conversation. Spend time with your new hire by sharing your story and letting them share theirs. A new person with new ideas and energy is a gift to an organization. These moments of high energy and curiosity are golden, so capture all the questions and thoughts during the critical first moments of building relationships. It's also a wonderful time for veterans to reaffirm their reason for showing up each day.

Your culture can grow and deepen with each new hire. Celebrate that process by creating rituals and customs that convey your organization's story and empower the newcomers to add their part. The new hire process actually demonstrates what is known as acculturation, but acculturation shouldn't be limited to just new hires. There are countless opportunities— basically, whenever you bring in new customers, projects, initiatives, products, and services—to include others in the process, creating a deeper experience, a shared wisdom and organizational resilience.

Culture Theater

Many companies don't put a lot of thought into culture at first. To them it's a paragraph in the employee handbook and a mission statement on their website. I've calculated that most organizations spend more on toilet paper each month than they do on their culture. Then leaders realize one day after reading the inflight magazine and think, *hey, we really need a company culture, because we're losing talent.* So they try to make up for lost time with hunting down best-place-to-work certifications to put on their website, email signatures, and the front door of the headquarters.

I witnessed and experienced a lot of theater trying to pass for genuine culture. This shows up as cosmetic window dressing, like ping-pong tables, Bosu ball chairs, kombucha bars, and the like—all meant to signify a hip, cutting-edge culture of innovation. Or it comes in the form of shortcuts packaged as "hacks" with assessments and clinical metrics. As if people are automatons.

You can't hack culture. You can't accelerate either with lunchtime yoga and corporate rope courses. Once more think about culture from its roots in cultivation. You can't fast-track a garden. You've got to nurture the soil and then tend to it with patience and care. It takes time.

Seemingly well-intentioned leaders fall into these traps when they focus solely on performance and related metrics of efficiency and execution. Yes, of course you want your company to perform better. But culture-driven change takes time to bear fruit. If you're looking for immediate results, you're just a part of the short-termism rampant on Wall Street these days, where companies sacrifice long-term strategy in order to bump up stock prices or quarterly earnings.

Later, we'll explore the difference between extrinsic and intrinsic motivation—and at how self-determined, internal motivation is a much more powerful driver of innovation and engagement. Performance and profit are an external motive. As a leader, your intrinsic motivation should be more about the human value of creating a worthy product or service— and about making your company a fulfilling place to work. That may sound corny, but we find that for the best leaders, creating an amazing work environment is a reward in itself, and not just a means to an end. As a leader, if you can make that pursuit your flow, your fulfillment zone, the rest begins to germinate and grow.

Finite Game vs. Infinite Game

I can't emphasize enough how a preoccupation with traditional performance metrics can kill culture. If your strategy is dictated entirely by short-term sales and earnings targets, you're playing what Simon Sinek calls a Finite Game. You're trying to cram the messy and volatile reality of life and business into the neat structure of quarterly financial statements. The Finite Game comes with a particular mindset. Finite players value stability and predictability above all else. They fear surprise, disruption, and uncertainty. Finite players, because they view the game as a zero-sum contest with clear winners and losers, also tend to eventually revert to self-interest. Their code is: what's best for me? That narrow framing, Sinek argues, leads directly into the decline of loyalty, trust, and engagement that we see at so many companies.[15]

---

[15] Sinek, Simon. *The Infinite Game.*

I have a background in economics. One of the godfathers of classical economic theory is John Maynard Keynes. He famously stated that "in the long run we are all dead" during a debate on restoring the pre-WWI fixed exchange rate system known as the gold standard. Keynesian economics is taught to every business student and MBA. Short-term thinking is baked into our understanding of economic and business systems and our leadership models. Partly because long-term thinking is hard to model and requires a different approach to understanding potential futures.

The other way is to choose to see business (and life) as an Infinite Game, or a long-run game, with just as many unknowns as knowns, no clear rules, no clear finish line. Infinite players embrace uncertainty and thrive amid disruption. They seek win-win solutions and create cultures of trust and risk-taking and innovation. Their code is: what's best for us?

"In the Infinite Game," Sinek writes, "the true value of an organization cannot be measured by the success it has achieved based on a set of arbitrary metrics over arbitrary time frames. The true value of an organization is measured by the desire others have to contribute to that organization's ability to keep succeeding."

He's describing a culture of connection, of belonging, of trust. These are the organizations that are resilient and able to weather difficult challenges. The COVID-19 pandemic has acted like a massive filter purging organizations holding onto the last vestiges of an old normal. Without massive cash reserves, even the most resilient company might not be able to survive a global pandemic for more than a year, but in their people, they hold the keys to restarting.

Craft a Distinctive Vision . . .

As you seek to articulate your organization's unique values and vision, don't settle for the generic and the cliché. Go deep. Be bold and put forth something truly distinctive and authentic. Invite others into the process. Aim for awe.

Unfortunately, most corporate value statements are so lacking in distinction you could literally swap them for another, and no one would notice. That's not hyperbole. A columnist at the *Financial Times* conducted an experiment with managers from two dozen companies. She read statements of values from company websites and asked managers to raise their hands when they recognized their own. Only five of the twenty-four managers correctly identified their own stated values.[16]

. . . But Remember That Culture Is Largely Unwritten

Amy Edmondson found it was a team's *unwritten* rules that were instrumental in creating psychological safety. And that was confirmed by Google's inquiry into its most successful teams.

Another way of looking at this is by considering the difference between *explicit* and *tacit* understanding. Explicit understanding is what we put down on paper and memorialize in documents. That's important because it gives us tools for preserving and transferring culture. And the mere act of putting values and vision into words puts us through a certain shared process of deliberation and consideration. Companies

---

[16] Kellaway, Lucy. "Hands up if you can say what your company's values are."

who think culture will just organically "happen" usually wake up one day and realize they have a culture problem.

But like an iceberg where we just see the tip above the water, the depth and staying power of culture is to be found in the unsaid, in the tacit. This understanding is rooted in relationships, in daily practice, in how people communicate and collaborate with one another. It can't fully be captured in words, and it certainly can't be captured in numbers. Organizations attempting to codify their culture in the employee manual undermine the living and ever-evolving nature of the human connection by reducing it to a single dimension.

It's like defining love. How often do people preface a definition of love with "words can't capture what it really means..." I'm not *against* writing cultural values down, but I'm against writing them down then treating them like checkbox items, or a monolith to be worshiped. Too often written documentation get stuffed into an intranet folder, becoming a static "whatever" as opposed to the living, breathing idea, and behavior that it should be.

In other words, culture is about human nature, and human nature is messy, emotional, irrational, and unpredictable. Trying to impose rigid performance metrics on culture doesn't account for all that messiness. There are products on the market that would argue this point. And maybe they do provide insights. But the tacit knowledge you have about culture is human phenomena. This is why the paying attention to small data is of paramount importance for building a healthy culture. How are people speaking to one another? Are they connecting or not connecting? Are they listening or not listening? What social cues are in our space? What are our memes?

Make Sure Everyone Has a Voice

A major part of human nature is the need to be heard, to be acknowledged, to be validated. And to have a role in authoring our own story—or contributing a verse.

That's why self-determination theory is the philosophical bedrock of ThirdSpace and the perspective from which I write this book. If your work environment isn't meeting those fundamental human needs of autonomy, mastery, and connection, your culture will have shallow roots at best.

Yes, leaders often must offer up the first iteration of a company's vision and values. But that should just be a humble opening volley in a back-and-forth process of co-creation. When people choose a path for themselves, they are far more committed and invested in seeing it through. That is the genuine ownership we talked about in the previous chapter.

Since culture ultimately requires dialogue, it is a humanistic process. As a leader, one of your greatest contributions can be to create and sustain an environment that fosters a healthy, inclusive conversation. It is your job as being higher on the org chart to clear a path for dialogues to happen and give air cover to those who would be targets of the corporate immune system trying to destroy something it perceives as a threat to the current power structure. If you won't assume this responsibility in your role, then leadership isn't your bag. As a leader it's your goal to execute a systematic process of letting go to a point where you aren't needed operationally. That means letting go of policy. Letting go of procedure. Letting of direct power. Letting go of assumed privilege.

Once that is done, (and frankly it never is) you will gain much more in return.

Keep It Simple

Culture stumbles and loses its way when it gets mired down in operational complexity, in data and metrics, in rules and policy, in business-as-usual and the status quo. We keep coming back to this idea of taking culture back to its roots, of stripping it down to its essentials. The previous chapters have boiled down to simple themes. Connection. Conversation. Trust. Safety.

If I had to boil this chapter down to one word, it would be this: human. Culture is a human process, one that must respect how real humans behave, feel, and think. Culture moves at the speed of that human process. The reality is that so much of what needs to be done in a business environment will take months and even years. This is difficult for management to grasp when their incentive structure is based on quarterly performance. Sorry, there's no quick fix.

MIT professor Donald Sull wrote a book called *Simple Rules: How to Thrive in a Complex World.* The theme of the book is (not surprisingly) straightforward: how simplicity trumps complexity in nature, business, and life. Running a company or organization can be complicated. Culture needs to be simple. (And simple is not the same as easy.)

Sull writes about how deceptively difficult it is to distill a philosophy into simple rules. He cites Michael Pollan, who summarized the nutritional insights of his book *The*

Omnivore's Dilemma as follows: "Eat food. Not too much. Mostly plants." An entire philosophy, right there in seven words. In the business world, take IDEO, whose culture is built around a distinctive approach to brainstorming guided by these simple rules: "Defer judgment. Encourage wild ideas. Go for quantity."

Distill your own organizational culture in three short phrases. Try not to exceed ten words total. Avoid abstract corporate-speak words like "synergy" and "leverage" and "existential." Think about creating rules or norms that guide and empower people, rather than policies that govern and restrict people. (It's the difference between mandating a customer service rep to request permission from a manager to give a customer a refund, and providing that rep with a guideline that empowers them to make the decision, one that does right by the customer, *without* having to consult management.)

As we frequently counsel at ThirdSpace, conceive of culture in terms of principles, not policies. Unfortunately, the management team at many companies, instead of thoughtfully crafting lasting foundational principles around how they want to treat each other and what is important as part of their belief system, gravitates to a rule book (aka the employee handbook) of punitive measures that anticipates all the ways an employee will do wrong. That's not how you should build culture. If you're not baking in trust as a guiding principle from day one, it's time to take a step back. Consider a new approach.

CHAPTER 4

How Do You Scale Culture?

> They always say time changes things, but you
> actually have to change them yourself.
>
> —Andy Warhol

As a business or organization moves from birth to childhood and then adolescence, it's a challenge to keep alive the initial spark that fired up the enterprise, while also allowing it to mature and evolve.

Your organization's growth—growth of employees, customers, revenue, geography, products, services—doesn't have to be exponential in order to make real demands of your culture. Think about it. What happens when a leader can no longer fit their team around a single table? Suddenly the magic ratio of seven direct reports to one leader breaks down. It's probably time to think about hiring a manager or cultivating one from within. You can kick the can down the road and just keeping bringing people on one at a time until you're absolutely forced to hire a manager. (This is what early stage companies are often forced to do.) But it could take weeks or even months to have an effective manager on board, and in the meantime, your culture might fray.

Each additional person you bring into your organization changes the chemistry, altering the culture equation. They are more than a role and a resume. They are a fully formed human being, with a unique set of experiences and point of view, complete with strengths and shortcomings. They will affect how you manage scaling.

Culture in your early days may have come together organically and spontaneously. As you grow, you can't leave the scaling of culture to chance. You have to be deliberate and have a strategy for passing culture on to newcomers, while at the same time giving them the chance to contribute to that culture. You don't want to squeeze your culture into an employee handbook or intranet, unless you want to ensure its death; much of what you need to pass on to others is unwritten. It can only be experienced. Think of how important oral traditions have been in the transmission of culture. An oral history is predicated on relationships and on human connection. That's precisely where your company's culture should live.

The abysmal employee onboarding process is also a lonely one. It puts new hires in the equivalent of a time-out corner, gripping the employee handbook. What if, instead, new employees were paired with a day-one mentor or coach who would serve as an ambassador of culture, tradition, and connection? What if that welcoming process went beyond a nickel tour guide for the first hour of their first day, with new hires paired long-term to an individual or team ensuring their comfort, success, and well-being?

Size and Structure: Is Flat the Way to Go?

When your workforce doubles and triples, you've got some big decisions to make about structure, and the flow of authority and decision-making—and these decisions in turn will go a long way toward shaping your culture.

You might assume that, once a business expands enough, it will reach a tipping point where the informal decision-making that may have ruled early on is no longer feasible. Indeed, for years this premise governed the business world. At a certain scale, you needed to "professionalize" the organization and embed its culture in established rules and procedures. However, startups that tried to perform a cultural U-turn and shift to a rules-based culture had a poor track record in surviving the 2008 financial crisis. If the culture that kickstarted your business got you to where you are today, don't assume it needs to be jettisoned entirely.

Ever since the 1980s, companies and management theorists have been exploring alternatives to the traditional command-and-control hierarchical model. Various theories and fashionable buzzwords have come and gone: the "networked" company, "matrix" organizations, etc. Now we have "holacracy" and "flat" organizations.

All of them are experiments in self-management—in giving authority and decision-making power directly to the teams and individual employees closest to the work at hand.

Before we consider the potential pitfalls of self-management, let's first look at the costs of the traditional hierarchical approach. Management consultant Gary Hamel has studied both models. In addition to the overhead costs of the bureaucratic model (where management can easily eat up 33% of your budget), there are three other costs:

1. Increased risk of large, calamitous decisions.
2. More approval layers and slower responses.
3. What Hamel calls the cost of tyranny: when you narrow the individual employee's scope of authority, "you shrink the incentive to dream, imagine, and contribute."[17]

Hierarchy's strength, on the other hand, is that it's great for maintaining *predictability* and *repeatability*. So if those qualities are at a premium in your line of business, maybe hierarchy is the way to go. But if your market is characterized by a rapidly changing environment, in which innovation and agility are key points of differentiation, you might want to build some degree of self-management or flatness into your organization.

Often the assumption is made that flat structures only work in startups, or small organizations. That's no longer the case. Automattic, the firm that created WordPress, employs a couple hundred people who all work remotely under a flat structure. GitHub is another internet company with a similar approach. All right, so you can get away with flat with knowledge work. But what about with manufacturing? Well, W.L. Gore is a multinational plastics manufacturer (best known for developing Gore-Tex) with over 10,000 employees

---

[17] Hamel, Guy. "First Let's Fire all the Managers."

and very little in the way of hierarchy. Or maybe you're thinking that, once you're locked into a bureaucratic model, you're stuck with it. The Brazilian conglomerate Semco, in response to a financial crisis that threatened its existence, changed course and committed itself to distributing decision-making to all its employees.

This is not a book about structure or organizational theory. But a basic premise of ThirdSpace is that culture is at least partly a matter of design. No, you don't design culture per se, just like you don't design love or relationships. But you can and should be deliberate in designing the principles and environment in which it grows and evolves. How you design a space—whether that space is virtual or in the real world—shapes the kind of conversations that naturally take place inside it. (Post-COVID-19, there's obviously going to be a lot of conversation around redesigning physical space for health reasons. It's also an opportunity to reexamine and carefully think through how that design affects culture.)

Similarly, your organization's structure—how authority and decision-making flow—will shape how employees talk and relate to one another formally and informally. Organizational structure is not just a question of execution and reporting. The organizational chart reveals what and who you value, who are the key points of connection. So put some thought and intention and effort into what path you want to take once it's time to scale your organization.

Consider how command-and-control authority and hierarchy operate in an organization like the military. It's highly effective in a time of crisis, but how does it affect creativity and purpose once the crisis is gone? Too many layers and policies create bureaucracy. At the other end of the spectrum is the Valve Corporation, a video game company that prides itself on being flat with minimal rules and policies. From the start, its culture was built to maximize creativity and openness. I encourage everyone to download Valve's version of an employee handbook. Whereas your typical handbook spells out rules and regulations, Valve's handbook—which is illustrated, almost like a comic book in some sections— highlights that all employees are empowered to bring their awesomeness to work and deploy it in any way they think is best for the company. The handbook may seem extreme, but...nobody can question Valve's success. Their model isn't for everyone, and it's not necessarily something you could retrofit to an existing company. But it's a reminder that you have a wide menu of options available to you.

Treat Middle Managers as More than Bureaucrats

If a more traditional, hierarchical approach is a better practical or philosophical fit for your company (or if that's just what you're stuck with for now), middle managers are often the missing link in creating an engaging and energizing workplace culture. Again, Gallup finds that the quality of middle management accounts for 70% of the variance in employee engagement.[18] There is a well-known expression that people don't quit their job, they quit their boss.

---

18 Wigert, Ben and Maese, Ellyn. "How Your Manager Experience Shapes Your Employee Experience."

While employees in general are too often not given an adequate voice in the creation of culture and are treated as mere cogs in the overall machinery, middle managers are a particularly undervalued and underutilized resource. It is all too easy to treat them as mere functionaries ensuring that the strategy and plans developed by senior leadership are executed quickly and efficiently. We should treat them as leaders in their own right.

In traditional organizations, the employee experience is largely shaped by the managerial experience. Engaged managers can drive an engaged workforce. So, says Gallup, "Make your managers your stars, not your scapegoats." Select them carefully and invest in them. Give them the training (and the trust and autonomy) appropriate to a group charged with developing the potential of your most valuable asset: your employees. Middle management positions are typically seen as just stepping-stones for further advancement. Give those ambitious employees another way to climb the ladder, and instead reserve middle management positions for those who truly have a calling to develop others.

Scaling Over Distance

For some organizations, growing in size also entails geographic growth, a scaling over distance: developing branch or satellite offices far from the core or founding team; or taking on individual employees in a remote capacity. With some companies, remote collaboration is built into the business model from day one.

In fact, one such case is part of the origin story of ThirdSpace. My partner Scott Jens was building a software company whose team was scattered over several states, with no shared office space. Maintaining a cohesive team wasn't a problem at first. But as the company grew to over two dozen employees, they outgrew the best available online options for remaining connected. They used a grab-bag of tools, but still—something was missing. Energy created during the annual company meeting fizzled as the year went on. Two dozen employees isn't a significant scaling in size. But when you combine it with distance, the challenges become significant.

It just so happened that Scott was continuing to work his day job at the time as an eye doctor, and that I happened to be one of his patients. We got to talking about organizational culture, and it turned out we shared some of the same fascinations. We began batting around the idea of a virtual water cooler, and those conversations evolved into ThirdSpace.

The technical term for an organization like SJ's software company is a *distributed workforce,* and it's an increasingly prevalent part of the present and future of work. According to one survey, 23% of remote workers say they are part of an entirely distributed workforce. This trend is obviously driven by technology, but there's a generational culture shift as well. Millennials are not nearly as wedded to the idea of going into the office; as many as 70% of young professionals view that traditional model as obsolete.

Recently, there have been some well-publicized cases of companies that switched to a remote workforce and saw significant gains in employee engagement. And suddenly there was a lot of talk about remote work being the solution to greater engagement. What some missed in their enthusiasm is that engagement numbers and remote work follow an S-curve. There is an increase in engagement that peaks but then bends back as people crave the face-to-face interaction. As a country, many have now experienced this feeling with "Zoom fatigue." Engagement peaks somewhere in the range of working remotely 60%–80% of the time, but then falls off significantly.[19]

Does that mean working remotely 100% of the time can't work? No. It just underscores how employees engaged in a mix of remote and on-site work get something incredibly valuable from those in-person interactions with their fellow employees coupled with the autonomy to work how they want to on their own. As *Time* has pointed out, the coronavirus outbreak has produced the world's largest work-from-home experiment. Almost overnight, remote work doubled from 31% of the workforce to 62%. Initially, a majority spoke positively about the experience, but that number tailed off as the weeks wore on.[20] People missed the way direct human connection energizes us.

Which brings us back to the virtual water cooler metaphor. The reason water cooler talk is so essential and powerful, and the reason why SJ and I immediately bonded over the concept, is that it is an end in itself. The point is simply connection for connection's sake. Small talk isn't pointless. Remember our earlier discussion of social cues? The trust-building social cues

---

[19] Hickman, Adam and Robison, Jennifer. "Is Working Remotely Effective?"

[20] Harter, Jim. "How Coronavirus Will Change the 'Next Normal' Workplace."

that seed great organizational culture communicate a simple message: *I am safe here.* Similarly, water cooler conversations built around connection as an end in itself also communicate a simple message: *We belong to the same tribe.*

Many organizations default to a pixie-dust promise of chat programs, HR systems, performance management tools, and project management platforms; but they don't create the kind of space inviting people connect on the deeper levels we discussed. They are fundamentally transactional. They're about achieving an objective, exchanging information, getting something done. In an emerging future of work where remote and distributed work will be the norm rather than the exception, leaders need tools to replicate the connectivity that happens around a water cooler. In the COVID-19 world, those working, teaching, and learning remotely will need more than just a transactional system designed around workflow. They will need a design for human connection.

Hire for Fit . . . or Adaptability?

> Self-actualizing people have the wonderful capacity to appreciate again and again, freshly and naïvely, the basic goods of life, with awe, pleasure, wonder, and even ecstasy, however stale these experiences may have become to others.
>
> —Abraham Maslow

Early decisions about who to hire or who to partner with tend to be made intuitively. Like my connection with SJ, they often happen organically and evolve out of mutual associations or previous collaborations. As an organization expands beyond its initial core team, however, leaders understandably become more deliberate about their hiring choices.

For years, the prevailing wisdom was to hire for so-called "cultural fit." Now there is good reason to question that wisdom.

The problem with the culture fit approach is that it can prompt us to hire people who remind us of ourselves. Researchers call the effect "looking-glass merit." This not only narrows the talent pool but can lead to a problematic lack of diversity. The hiring process is fraught with potential unconscious bias in the first place, and hiring for fit opens the door for even more of that bias.

A lack of diversity undermines culture in several ways. It's not just a PR or public image issue—although that's nothing to scoff at. (Silicon Valley tech companies are famously obsessed with culture but simultaneously have a real diversity and inclusion problem. A "bro culture" is one thing when you're working out of your basement or garage with your best friends from college. It's another when you're a publicly traded company with hundreds or even thousands of employees.) A lack of diversity, whether along lines of race, gender, or other measures, is also a lack of cognitive and experiential diversity. Diverse teams tend to be more innovative, and they better reflect the markets they're trying to appeal to.

Facebook and other companies are now publicly distancing themselves from the idea of culture fit. Pandora has embraced the alternative approach of seeking "culture adds."

Amir Goldberg of the Stanford Business School has researched culture fit and found that it's a mixed bag when it comes to performance. A culture fit may benefit both employee and employer in the short term. But in the long term, what seems to matter more is adaptability—or what Goldberg calls *enculturability*. He defines enculturability as "the ability to adapt by reading and interpreting subtle social cues."[21]

Again, those social cues—they're critically important. The heart and soul of a culture are embodied in unwritten rules, in the minutiae of how people interact daily. It's the people who can intuit that "small data" who will thrive and mesh with the company in the long run. And their adaptability will ensure that they will evolve with the culture as it evolves.

That adaptability should be a two-way street. The individual employee must be flexible and bend to the arc of the organization's growth trajectory. But so too should the organization create space and freedom for the individual's growth trajectory.

Which brings us back to self-determination theory and why it is a cornerstone for this book and for ThirdSpace. That theory, and the related theory of flow, posit a growth cycle in which, as we gain mastery over a task or craft, we will (as long as we are autonomous and intrinsically motivated) naturally seek higher challenges to stretch and test our abilities. The best cultures are cognizant of that individual growth cycle, even as they expand and take on new employees. Hiring those who don't fit, but who exhibit

---

21 Walsh, Dylan. "Look Beyond 'Culture Fit' When Hiring."

qualities of neuroplasticity, push the rest of us to grow as individuals and organizations.

The Ultimate Goal: Resilience

Organizations that create an environment in which employees can consistently work in that "flow zone" will themselves be in organizational flow. They will have attained a collective adaptability, otherwise known as resilience.

This is what scaling culture is ultimately about: evolving over time in size, complexity, geographic reach, and diversity— while retaining the nimbleness and vitality that made the company great in the first place. As we are experiencing as a nation, resilience is now more critical than ever. Resilient organizations embody all the qualities we've discussed to this point, and they possess the ability to thrive in the uncertain environment ahead.

Some established companies mistakenly assume they are "too big to fail" or have been around so long they have seen just about everything the world and markets can toss at them. This rigid thinking will be their undoing, and the increasing pace of the demise of F500 companies is proof. The future lies with the nimble, adaptable organizations possessing an Aikido-like ability to utilize and capitalize on exogenous forces rather than clumsily trying to bludgeon markets with brute force. Underpinning this ability to change: the culture, and the diverse teams who make up that culture.

CHAPTER 5

How Do You Change Culture?

The best time to plant a tree was twenty years ago.
The second best time is now.

—Chinese Proverb

Let's say you've done a reasonably good job at the actions we've discussed in the preceding chapters. You seeded culture by establishing trust and connection; you made it sustainable by incorporating shared values into behavior and being mindful of your norms and unwritten rules; then you scaled it as your company expanded in size and scope.

But then you come to a different crossroads. Maybe you got complacent and the company's culture grew stale, and young and hungry companies are threatening your market share. Maybe technological disruption renders a product line obsolete and you must retool and reinvent, and you know you won't get there unless you also reboot the culture. Maybe a crisis upends the entire economy.

Or maybe you never really paid attention to culture. You talked about it, but it wasn't a daily priority, or it was delegated to HR and not seen as a leadership issue. You counted on culture to grow organically on its own. And now something has happened, forcing a realization that it doesn't develop into a positive force if left to its own.

However you come to that crossroads, you know you've got to change and shake up your culture. Is this possible? Can a tiger change its stripes?

Yes . . . but it's difficult. More often than not, business leaders fail in this effort. In part because they want the seven-minute-abs version of cultural change. This journey may take years because it took years to create the problem. From experience working with companies who are motivated to shift culture, at ThirdSpace we've seen evidence for early changes within two to three months. This doesn't mean unicorns, rainbows, and glitter everywhere. It means someone is testing the waters to establish the seeds of trust.

Over two decades of studies and surveys have come back with virtually the same conclusion: only about 30% of change programs succeed.[22] That's a staggering rate of failure. Only as a hitter in Major League Baseball can you fail more than two-thirds of the time and be considered a success.

Why is changing culture so hard?

And what's the key to those companies that get change right?

Avoid the Trap of Business as Usual

Culture and change are deeply connected, and culture isn't static. So it must be evolving and malleable to those who are part of it. Like all leaders, you want to foster a strong culture

---

[22] Lyons, Rich. "Three Reasons Why Culture Efforts Fail."

so your company will be innovative and dynamic, able to adapt to the times, and even be at least one step ahead of the curve. And if you're trying to create change in response to an external threat or disruption in your market, you know you can't do so without a culture that embraces change and growth and learning.

Writing in the *Harvard Business Review* about why even good companies can't rise to the challenge of change, Donald Sull of the MIT Sloan School of Management identifies what he calls "active inertia." We usually think of inertia in terms of physics describing a moving object's tendency to persist in its current trajectory. Organizations have inertia as well, whether that's a default to the status quo, total inaction, or being stuck despite good intentions.

Sull writes that in the business world, active inertia "is an organization's tendency to follow established patterns of behavior—even in response to dramatic environmental shifts. Stuck in the modes of thinking and working that brought success in the past, market leaders simply accelerate all their tried-and-true activities. In trying to dig themselves out of a hole, they just deepen it."

What happens to companies, Sull says, is that a previous winning formula becomes a rut. Ways of thinking and approaching problems that were once fresh and fluid become rigid and fixed. Dynamic values become dogmas, a devotion to the status quo.[23]

There is an even more insidious type of inertia where certain people or roles within organizations actively work to

---

[23] Sull, Donald. "Why Good Companies Go Bad."

preserve existing problems because they perceive themselves as the solution. This was coined as the Shirky Principle by author Clay Shirky. Individuals, departments, and entire institutions develop a vested interest in perpetuating the very problems they profess they want to solve.

I've often criticized human resource departments as enablers of the pathology within organizations. They should be department leading the charge for change. Yet somewhere along the way, HR lost its core purpose of supporting the humans with resources, and instead became a centrifuge of indolence with the sole purpose of protecting the corporate nest. Their marching orders are "Make sure we don't get sued!"

I know that's a harsh assessment. But I'm not the only one making that call, as demonstrated by the DisruptHR Movement. (Not a very effective movement, in my view— but its mere existence reflects widespread recognition of the problem.) I've experienced this lethargic and anemic corporate pathology again and again, observing professionals trained and responsible for personnel and cultural development claiming to be "too busy" to do anything meaningful about it. Too busy, eh? Doing what? Sure, lots of meetings. Lots of processes. Lots of emails . . . there are always emails. The changing world and the competition don't care about paperwork, and they will take your lunch money.

Organizations can expend months and even years trying to strategize some perfect plan on paper, and the thicker the plan, the better. Meanwhile, the world is changing. They are missing opportunities, hemorrhaging talent, and losing time. Management is left slack-jawed when disruption bears down upon them. They've been so busy for ages with low-value activity that they never see the meteor coming. There never seems to be enough time or resources to invest in proactive strategies; but somehow, after the storm, there are resources to clean it all up, and everyone finds religion—at least for a little while.

Once a business has grown through their early stages of defining their business model and delivering it consistently, the business becomes a "going concern" in the parlance of accountants. Therefore, developing each person to their fullest, so they can build the culture of innovation and deliver higher meaning, is the only thing that matters. Everything else is superfluous. Claiming otherwise means someone is hiding behind process and bureaucracy because the real effort resembles something like hard work.

It is scary and difficult, and you might fail. Own it. You might be emboldened when you experience the support thrown behind someone willing to walk the line. Focusing on your culture will serve your employees, your customers, your efficiency, your product defects, your innovation, and your deeper mission.

It may sound like I see culture as the hammer, and therefore everything else in the organization is a nail. Okay, then change my mind. What other effort can leadership undertake that could provide such a broad and deep return on investment? I've seen companies dump millions on ERP systems, which only excites some IT folks and the salespeople who sold it. Zero value (by value, I'm referring to the pillars of self-determination theory: autonomy, mastery, and connection) was created for employees, which then yielded nothing for the customer. Again, more budget was allocated for toilet paper than invested into creating a place where people love to work.

Culture Change Gone Wrong

Companies that attempt culture change without an authentic commitment to breaking with business as usual fail. One interesting such failure is GM's now defunct Saturn brand. The intention was good, and they had a mission to rally around. However, the distinctive Saturn organization, brand, and culture never had an organic connection with the rest of the company. Instead of being a culture laboratory that might have triggered company-wide change, Saturn instead became a dissonant bolt on to GM. GM might have been better off directly addressing the internal problems versus trying to spin them out. Rising as a phoenix from the flames only works if you burn the old edifice down. Trying to be like somebody else (like the Japanese automakers in this case) was untenable. This raises the question: should organizations spin off, and if so, should they unlever from the parent organization? Keeping ties has its own issues because the spin-off (like Saturn) lives in the shadow of the parent and never quite establishes its own culture. If spin-offs are the most effective way to change, it foretells an unfortunate future for the parent organization.

Change rarely works unless it's an authentic effort undertaken by the entire organization. If this is done for politics, optics, branding, or marketing, without substance or depth, then the truth will find a way out. A false effort will rot your organization and erode your brand, and recovery will be extremely difficult. You'll hemorrhage customers and talent. Take United Airlines TED, a poorly conceived attempt to mimic Southwest. I flew on TED once, but flying in the hold of a cargo plane would have been a better experience. What TED accomplished was taking an already horrible experience of flying coach and discovering a way to make it worse. TED emulated Southwest's design, planes, uniforms, food, and flight logistics, but it died a quick death. Beneath the surface changes, United Airlines was still going about business the way they'd always done. TED was a botched facelift on an old crone, and the culture was never created to embody an authentic change.

The larger question is this: can established companies—especially early to mid-20th century companies—truly reinvent themselves as demonstrated through their culture? In many cases, the jury is still out on their efforts. In my home state of Wisconsin, we have a stronghold of insurance companies. Many are over eighty years old but have come to realize their old-school industry is under siege from multiple forces. They have responded with innovation teams, venture teams, traditional mergers and acquisitions, and attempts to align with the startup community. Some have built amazing new buildings as an outward expression of their innovative thinking. There is no shortage of activity that signals change might be happening, but is it substantive change to the DNA of their culture? Having walked the halls of the parent organizations, I get mixed signals where it feels like business as usual, so perhaps there is an acknowledgment that the old bastions aren't going to be the primordial soup for cultural change and innovation. Instead, it requires a distancing from the parent in order to survive the inevitable prolicide.

Menasha Corp in Central Wisconsin is another case in point. The company started in 1849 as a wooden bucket manufacturer. There isn't a large market for wooden buckets anymore, so you'd expect a company this narrowly focused to have folded up long ago. But the founders were quick to adapt, which accounts for why it remains one of oldest and largest privately held companies in the U.S. Their product innovations, focus on corporate responsibility, stewardship of the environment, and community are impressive. They have a wind farm in front of their LEED Gold Certified headquarters. They work to reduce water waste. They reprocess plastic and recycle most of their cardboard. Menasha has changed its stripes, more than once—and those cultural shifts have been broad and deep, clearly woven into the DNA of the company. They have played the Infinite Game and have utilized a range of strategies to not only be relevant but lead by example.

Less Is More

We talked about how some previously energetic startups, once they hit a certain stage of growth, attempt to institutionalize culture in the form of rules and procedures—and how this approach to sustaining and scaling culture usually backfires. Across the board, it seems that the companies that do succeed in changing culture for the better do so by stripping away policies and rules and procedures. They replace bureaucracy with meaningful freedom and autonomy for their employees.

A striking example is Netflix, which rode the dot-com wave of the late 1990s until that bubble went bust. The 9/11 attacks dealt a second blow to the economy, and Netflix had to lay off a third of their employees. But a curious thing happened. The layoffs also forced the company to let go of a lot of managers and cut back on bureaucracy, and the remaining employees, although overworked, also experienced a newfound freedom. Ever since, the company has been engaged in a running experiment of giving employees increased freedom paired with increased responsibility.[24] The bet has paid off. Rather than having an army of middle management as enforcers of policies, employees were trusted to self-manage. This is a powerful display of trust, albeit born out of necessity to survive.

Former Netflix chief talent officer Patty McCord sums up the approach with radical simplicity: "Be honest and treat people like adults." The company did away with performance reviews, a set vacation time, and formal travel and expense procedures. Employees are trusted to take time off when they need it. The company's expense policy is five words long: "Act in Netflix's best interests." Empowering autonomy in this manner is the ultimate expression of trust. Old school managers might say that this would never work at their organizations because people would cheat. That cynicism produces a workforce of clock-watchers who, as George Carlin said, "Work just enough to not get fired and get paid just enough not to quit."

Ricardo Semler did the same thing with Semco in Brazil. He joined the company in 1980, twenty-seven years after his father founded it. Within a couple of years, the company was on the brink of bankruptcy, forcing a major reassessment of their way of doing business. They threw the old management rules out the window and replaced them with a culture built on three simple principles: workplace democracy, profit-sharing,

---

[24] McCord, Patty. "How Netflix Reinvented HR."

and informational transparency. Instead of hierarchy, they have interconnected, self-managed teams. Semler replaced an organizational pyramid with circles.

"The organizational pyramid is the cause of much corporate evil because the tip is too far from the base. Pyramids emphasize power, promote insecurity, distort communications, hobble interaction, and make it very difficult for the people who plan and the people who execute to move in the same direction."

Like Netflix's Patty McCord, Semler engaged in addition by subtraction. "One of my first moves when I took control of Semco was to abolish norms, manuals, rules, and regulations." Employees establish their own budgets and production schedules.[25]

There's a myth that dispensing with rules and hierarchy only works for small, funky startups. Semco is one of Brazil's most profitable manufacturing companies. Rosabeth Moss Kanter of the Harvard Business School has studied how giant, well-established companies can succeed with a modified version of this approach. Companies like IBM, Proctor & Gamble, and Cisco might not engage in cultural change as ambitious as the efforts at Netflix and Semco, but the underlying spirit is the same:

> "The global giants we studied are operating according to a model that differs from what most people might expect of a multinational corporation. It is not ironfisted hierarchy or some clever

---

[25] Semler, Ricardo. "Managing Without Managers."

engineering of structure that provides coherence to their organizations; it is the effect of commonly held values translating into operations through clear standards and processes—values and standards that are embraced by individuals because they allow autonomy, flexibility, and self-expression."[26]

The cynical person will point out that moving from a pyramid structure to a circle a la knights of the roundtable is just more theater. I agree that in many organizations it is that at best. Examples where this seems to be most prevalent is in the movement toward agile business processes. It typically starts off with a senior manager attending some conference or off-site training. They cook up an action plan. Then a small team does the agile rituals and obtains a new tracking software, and they now stand up at meetings. Then it is clumsily pushed out into the rest of the department. While on paper they shifted a reporting structure from a pyramid to a circle, it's more of the same. They never took the time to build trust and understand continuous delivery of value (aka their values never changed), and managers still see it as their role to police the agile teams. Frankly, it terrifies the management that they can't be judge and jury in the room any longer. Ultimately, they create a bastardized and ineffective mutant form of management, with new forms of documentation and overhead, that barely adopts the mechanics of agile and never gets to the ethos of why it emerged in the first place.

---

[26] Kanter, Rosabeth Moss. "Transforming Giants."

Freedom Within a Framework

Obviously, total employee freedom with zero structure would result in chaos. Since an organization was formed to fulfill a specific purpose or business mission, it requires guardrails to focus energy in productive, strategic ways. In other words, that freedom needs to sit within a framework—some kind of "glue" that holds the organization together and keeps it coherent.

And that's where leaders face a fundamental choice. You can establish that framework via elaborate rules and procedures, and a rigid command-and-control hierarchy. Or that framework can consist largely of shared values and behaviors, grounded in broad but flexible principles.

A modern example of principles can be found on Amazon's corporate site. Whether you think Amazon lives these principles is your decision, but that's true of many organizations. They create manifestos but then fail to carry them out.

- Customer Obsession
- Ownership
- Invent and Simplify
- [Leaders] Are Right, A Lot
- Learn and Be Curious
- Hire and Develop the Best
- Insist on the Highest Standards
- Think Big
- Bias for Action
- Frugality
- Earn Trust

- Dive Deep
- Have Backbone; Disagree and Commit
- Deliver Results

Choosing culture as your framework allows you to maximize employee autonomy, self-determination, mastery, and fulfillment.

The path you take with your organization really depends on a basic balancing act. Organizations must deliver a degree of both *reliability* and *adaptability*. There is a creative tension between the two, a kind of yin and yang. Every leader and every organization will solve that equation differently. A software company might skew more toward agility and flexibility, while a traditional manufacturing company might require more reliability and stability. Organizations in highly regulated industries face other constraints and legal requirements, but those constraints are not an excuse to settle for business as usual. There can still be infinite possibilities within a box.

As Kanter and others have documented, a handful of large, established companies have been successful at placing a premium on an inclusive, democratic workplace culture devoted to employee self-determination. Even the military—historically defined by a rigid hierarchy—has in the post-9/11 era embraced a more fluid, self-managed team approach to special operations. General Stanley McChrystal's "Team of Teams" model has in fact emerged as an influential approach to being adaptable in a complex world with hard constraints. Team of Teams creates a formal cultural and operational framework, but one that is fluid enough to adapt to changing conditions. It empowers the team members closest to the customer to make decisions and rapidly report up information to personnel handling strategy.

A Team of Teams culture is a powerful structure. It implies a deep sense of autonomy balanced with accountability. Will it work for all organizations, though? My Spidey sense says no. (I wonder, for instance, how it would apply to a company that generates creative products, such as physical or performance art.)

The freedom that animates authentic cultural change is never going to be real if leaders attempt to rigidly control and dictate the path forward. Leaders must be open to new insights, and to the testing of old assumptions. If you poll an audience at a typical HR conference, they'll say culture starts with leadership. But that's a mistake. There are elements that only leadership can provide, sure. But meanwhile, the in-the-trenches culture is constantly bubbling up. It needs to be validated, understood, and embraced. That bottom-up process is a sign of vitality, and it's incumbent on all within the organization to build the connection between the layers. If the numerous layers are getting in the way, listen to that signal. Consider removing the layers because the signal attenuates and obfuscates with each hop it needs to make— just like the old game of telephone.

At a basic, granular level, cultural shift is about discovery: discovery of self, of your colleagues and employees, of the living, evolving culture you share. This is a model of an organization as a living organism, not a machine. Discovery, possibility, and curiosity are the flames that must be kept alive. Not snuffed out by a preoccupation with control and predictability.

CHAPTER 6

Who Owns Culture?

Life's most persistent and urgent question is: "What are you doing for others?"

—Martin Luther King Jr.

All the world's a stage, and *all the men and women merely players;* they have their exits and their entrances; and one man in his time plays many parts.

—Shakespeare

A thousand candles can be lighted from the flame of one candle, and the life of the candle will not be shortened. Happiness can be spread without diminishing that of yourself.

—Gandhi

First, a confession. The title of this chapter is a trick question.

But for the sake of argument, as a kind of thought exercise, let's answer the question narrowly and see how a few different scenarios might play out.

In one scenario—and this has traditionally been the situation for many businesses—senior leadership owns the culture. At some level, this makes sense. They may own the business, so why shouldn't they own the culture? In some cases, they may have even founded the company; so why not have them be the shapers and keepers of the culture? The problem, of course, is that this lends itself to a strong top-down dynamic. Leaders can make all the pronouncements they want to about the company being inclusive and valuing the contribution of all employees. But if culture—the organization's purpose and reason for being—are seen as emanating from the corner office or the C-suite, those words will ring hollow. And measures like employee engagement will remain mired in mediocrity. Having a particular leader own the culture can introduce a dynasty problem where the next person to assume the role doesn't carry the same kind of charisma. Tim Cook is good CEO, but he isn't Steve Jobs. Steve Balmer was a bombastic wrecking ball for Microsoft when he took over as CEO.

So let's imagine the opposite scenario, where employees own the culture. Democracy in action! While such a situation may have some appeal in theory, in practice, it breaks down. Major strategic decisions still fall on senior leadership. Strategy and culture won't be properly aligned without their guidance. You'll also have a high likelihood of fragmentation as various fiefdoms and cliques emerge in the absence of a firm hand at the wheel.

A third option would be to designate middle management as the ambassadors of culture. There is a powerful kernel of wisdom to this approach, since middle management plays a key role in serving as a bridge between senior leadership and rank-and-file employees; engaged managers lead to an engaged workforce. But for culture to be strong and robust, it must evolve and change, and middle management typically doesn't have the authority to enact such change.

So it appears there are strong arguments to be made for culture not being owned at the top, middle, or bottom of an organization. We could propose some hybrid of ownership structure, but that might come with extra complexity and inherent communication downsides.

So what if we're approaching this question the wrong way? There are any number of organizational models to rearrange the deck chairs, and for many, that is all restructuring is. What if the idea of "ownership" and a structure of ownership is flawed? If we approach ownership differently, then perhaps the organizational structure will become clearer.

Redefining Ownership

It is folly to view culture as belonging to just one set of actors in an organization. If culture is alive and truly the lifeblood of the company, the air that everyone who works there breathes, then it becomes a part of every employee, executive, and manager, regardless of status. And ideally, a part of everyone makes its way into the culture.

But there is another way in which it does make sense to talk about ownership and culture. It's not about possession of something ephemeral. It's more akin to a stewardship. This is ownership as emotional investment, as "buying into" the mission and values of a company. When the organization we work for aligns with our own values, we have a stake in its success, almost as if we actually did own it. We take the work personally. It becomes more than a job. It's part of our mission and our sense of meaning.

Here, ownership isn't a zero-sum game where my ownership comes at the expense of someone else's. This isn't ownership as status, but as behavior and philosophy. When we talk about "taking ownership," it has nothing to do with splitting up a pie. It's about showing initiative, about pride, and about accountability. When people own a property, they "pick up the garbage" and take responsibility for their space. Beyond the legal construct, they make a personal connection to that place, and they tend it and build upon it. The same is true for culture. But for that emotional investment to be fully and concretely realized, participants must be empowered to contribute and make it their own.

This process begins well before you hire anyone new. Your cultural impact should radiate out into the community. It should be the front door for prospective new hires and be a guide for an employee's journey. If you're currently trying to hammer new hires into some mold, you are assimilating people, yes, like the Borg, not acculturating them. This means any efforts related to maintaining and "owning" culture will feel like extra work on top of their job description. Employees who get extra work assigned often require a different set of incentives because the emotional buy-in is so low, and the company is eating into things the employees actually care about, such as family and personal time.

At one company I consulted at, the managing director was worried about pressure from the corporate office due to the scathing Glassdoor reviews. They formed an employee relations committee and people were "voluntold" to participate. The office had around forty staff members, so the cultural issues were well known, widely discussed among the rank-and-file, but management actively worked on a cover-up. The employee relations committee was supposed to act like a glee squad, sprinkling joy and frivolity around the office. If you didn't comply, you went on a secret naughty list and were labeled as a malcontent. Ultimately, an HR file was created so they could terminate with minimal fear of legal complications. Social gatherings were held, usually with half or fewer employees joining in, and the gatherings were awkward. People would pound drinks, pay obligatory homage to the directors, and then split. Side conversations centered on gossip related to how messed up the company was.

This was an abysmal failure on multiple levels. It was systemic rot from top to bottom. Directors were insincere about caring for culture. They delegated to an ad hoc committee where the focus was on merrymaking, without seriously addressing real issues. Rank-and-file employees had zero power and knew that speaking out would make them a target. The corporate office C-suite was a citadel of former lawyers. They wanted a stock pump to retire on and would rain down corporate legal on anyone who tried to speak up. As a consultant, you can quickly assess if an organization has the right attitude about change and the aptitude to make it happen. This company had neither. It was a nightmare . . . and they continue to hemorrhage people. The only reason they're still able to hire newcomers is that the turnover is so massive there are no old timers around to relay the sordid history.

The Employee Experience

Employees are unlikely to display initiative, pride, and accountability when they don't feel connected to the organization. Employee engagement numbers that hover around 35% are just one indication that such disconnection is more the rule than the exception. This stat has held true year after year despite all the new-fangled HR Information Systems, organizational consultants, and laughable "best place to work" certifications.

In response to these poor numbers (and to the high turnover rates that go with them), HR professionals (and, more precisely, organizational development professionals) have in recent years started talking about "the employee experience" instead of employee engagement. It's not just a matter of semantics. It's a holistic way of looking at a career, the flawed concept of work-life balance, and what it means to us. I'd push that even further and say we have to look at the *human* experience as it pertains to our work. We aren't just employees, especially when the lines of work blur and our work-related duties enter our personal time.

It goes to the heart of one of the philosophical foundations of ThirdSpace: self-determination theory.

Thus far, I've danced around this concept because it's a mouthful. But at its core, it's a simple idea. Self-determination theory grew out of the study of motivation—specifically, the difference between intrinsic and extrinsic motivation. When we act based on external factors and rewards (rules, authority, money, fame), we may be competent and at times even excel, but we will rarely put our heart and soul into something.

Intrinsic motivation is far more powerful. When we act because of our own values, interests, curiosities, and passions, it's almost as if the activity (whether it's a hobby or our job) becomes its own reward. You don't need external incentives or motivators other than the activity itself. The psychologist Mihaly Csikszentmihaly called this a state of "flow," one "in which people are so involved in an activity that nothing else seems to matter." In sports we call it being "in the zone." Regardless of whether it's in sports, or an artistic pursuit, or our paid employment, Csikszentmihaly found that being in this state leads not just to better results and superior performance, but to increased happiness, well-being, and fulfillment.[27]

You may be thinking that when you're paid to do a job, your salary is, by definition, an external reward. Point taken. But what self-determination theory discovered was that under the right conditions, we can internalize extrinsic motivation and essentially convert it to intrinsic motivation. Yes, we're getting paid, and we still want our health insurance and our 401(k). But if the work aligns with our values and our sense of self, it also becomes its own reward. It becomes a kind of self-expression. Another way to look at our wages, salaries, and benefits is as validation of value. Yes, we obviously value being able to pay our bills, but we also value the feeling of knowing our contribution matters so much that someone is willing to demonstrate their gratitude (in this case, through wages).

---

[27] Csikszentmihaly, Mihaly. *Flow: The Psychology of Optimal Experience.*

Here's a test. Ask yourself if employees would do their jobs at your company if they weren't paid. That is to say, they volunteered to be there. Another way of thinking about that is they show up each and every day because they want to, not because they must. What would your company look like if it was comprised of people with the attitudes of volunteers who showed up because they *wanted* to? Workforce laws aside, maybe a goal would be creating the type of culture that moves motivations from "have to participate," across the continuum towards "want to participate."

One technique potentially linking extrinsic rewards with feelings of intrinsic motivation is offering stock options in a company. For many, stock options feel like flimsy monopoly money because you never get to exercise the options, but others see it as real ownership. As a startup founder, we had stock agreements with our early employees because we couldn't pay them market rates. In addition, I wanted them to feel a deeper connection to what we were building. Offering ownership could be a path to igniting that feeling. I knew the startup life is tough and demands a lot of time, energy, intellectual property, and emotions before it properly rewards you financially. Therefore, the incentive of ownership turned *my* vision into *our* vision that we were building together. Even with that incentive, it didn't motivate employees on a daily level the way I expected. Yet, if there was a change to the amount, value or vesting timeline it was interesting how much they advocated for their own position and contribution to the organization.

What are the right conditions for self-determination theory to activate and motivate? Research since the 1960s has shown (and my personal experience supports this) that people have three universal human needs: the need for connection; for autonomy; and for mastery, or in other words, competence. An environment that meets these needs creates a primordial soup in which people can experience the fire in their belly kindled, white hot. Dan Pink has created a popular real-time sketch presentation on this topic on YouTube.

You as a business leader have the power to create an environment, that primordial soup, that either supports or thwarts these basic needs. That in a nutshell is what culture is all about as it relates to a fulfilling employee experience. When you are about to create some new policy or procedure, run it through those filters and ask others to do so as well. It's an easy litmus test for determining whether the action you are about to take creates more connection, less connection, or about the same. Does it have the power to increase a feeling of autonomy, decrease it, or keep it at about the same level? Can it help the employee journey toward mastery, or does it hamper it?

It's not easy it hit all three targets. And there may be trade-offs. But it's worth it to give it a try next time you're about to roll out the next big thing or propose a new initiative.

Culture, or Cultures?

Another problem with even asking the question of who owns culture is the assumption that culture is a single, monolithic entity. In most organizations, you can experience distinct subcultures. That diversity can be a weakness and a problem if not understood and correctly channeled. But if your subcultures are embraced and celebrated and openly addressed, they can be a strength leading to achieving the business goals that leadership is always grappling to attain.

Take a fine dining restaurant. As anyone who has worked at such an establishment knows, there is a clear distinction between the kitchen culture and the front-of-the-house culture. In the front where customers dine, the wait staff move with quiet precision. The kitchen where the food is made is often a scene of barely controlled chaos, with the chef barking commands and the cooks scrambling to keep up with orders. Employees joke about these two very different subcultures. But at well-run restaurants they complement one another, and ownership makes a concerted effort to bring them together for all-staff meals.

But such a symbolic show of unity isn't enough. Complementary teams and subcultures must come to understand and appreciate how much they rely on one another and learn to trust that. A restaurant's wait staff are also the chef's eyes and ears, giving those who prepare the meals insight into how they are being received by diners. And wait staff can better enhance a diner's appreciation of the food when they communicate closely with the cooks and understand exactly how and why a meal is prepared the way it is.

The late chef Charlie Trotter often described his restaurant as an improvisational jazz session in which two riffs will never be the same. The dynamics between the chefs, staff, and guests were something Trotter was known for, along with his intensity. The result was an experience of food, culture, flavor, and art that was world renowned. Having dined at Charlie Trotter's in Chicago, I can attest to the subcultures of the restaurant in addition to the way it even spread out into the Lincoln Park neighborhood. If you decided mid-meal to try a different item from their menu, the staff would relay that information to the chef so they could complement the flavor profiles of subsequent orders. Without asking, the sommelier might deliver a new wine to augment your experience. When I dined there, we had tickets for a live Second City show that started at 10 p.m. The staff made sure we were able to get to the show on time, and we were offered a chance to come back afterward for our dessert. It wasn't just dine and get out. They extended the experience and blended with our plans.

What if your business could respond that quickly and effectively to the unknown?

That unique customer experience doesn't emerge from command and control hierarchy, despite Charlie's intensity and desire for perfection. The team was like a jazz band, and you could tell they enjoyed their jam. It was an intense environment but one of powerful learning and experiences.

Similarly, at tech companies, engineers are often a distinct subculture unto themselves. Other subcultures will naturally emerge based on department, gender, job role, shift, physical location, age, seniority, or any number of other factors. These various cultures can be positive, and they can be sources of discontent. Most of them emerge organically and for a reason. Each subculture will have its own norms, and its natural leaders who are stewards of that culture. If those leaders are also respected as a voice in the larger operation, they will see themselves as stewards of the organization as a whole, and work to bridge any differences with other teams and their subcultures.

It is only when a subculture feels ignored or dismissed or unappreciated that resentment and divisiveness take root. As a leader you need to understand the genesis of those subcultures, the positive aspects and the negatives. If you listen not just to understand, but also to empower those subcultures to act on their beliefs and insights, you can achieve incredible shifts in your culture and capabilities as an organization.

If this is a new approach for leadership in an established organization, they will need to wade into this slowly, taking the time to build trust and open the doors for dialog. Coming too hot and fast will cause subcultures to circle the wagons in survival mode and put the senior management at odds with them.

An example: one company, where I was made interim COO, made educational video games for children. You would expect that organization to be fun and full of energy, but when I started consulting there, it was the complete opposite. This young company carried a very strange, heavy vibe, and you could hear a pin drop in the office on most days.

Three friends founded the organization. In spite of themselves and their collective arrogance, they managed to keep it going mainly because game developers are so passionate about what they do that they will tolerate an unfortunate amount of abuse to keep creating what they love. Part of the issue at this organization was that rank-and-file were paid barely-living wages with minimal to no benefits while the three founders squirreled away profits.

I performed an analysis of wages versus market, and it was almost shameful what some of the employees were being paid . . . yet the three founders felt it was justified and equitable. The

CEO once claimed they "rescued" one of the artists from Target; now, she was now being paid for doing something she actually liked. He didn't claim this artist should be paying *them* for the privilege of working there, but that was implied by the other sacrifices the employees made on behalf of the organization, which ultimately only benefited the three founders.

I had frequent conversations and coaching sessions with the founders to shift their thinking. They were on the cusp of losing their talent, but they had no idea of the horrific culture they had created.

After a coaching session one morning, the CEO walked into the office acting all chipper and jovial like Ebenezer Scrooge on Christmas Day. I had an early meeting with him. So we sat down in the sole conference room, and he proudly announced, "What can I do for you today, Scott?" The delivery was so rehearsed and saccharine that I had to forcibly restrain myself. Not much will cause me to raise an eyebrow, but I was mortified that he was using this bit on his employees. He actually thought this would be helpful. Instead of opening doors to a conversation, it was felt like the CEO playing a mind game. Given the power dynamics present in that small office, employees only sank lower in their seats and turned the music up on their headphones.

Culture as Conversation

If we continue to look at the role of leadership in culture less in terms of ownership or possession, and more in terms of creating an environment that supports universal human needs, it seems we are talking more about *stewardship* than anything else. We've used that term several times because it conveys how the culture belongs to everyone, and everyone belongs to the culture. A steward plays a leadership role but it isn't necessarily permanent. With the name it is implied that a steward may play a limited contribution before handing over the mantle to another. It is your job as a leader to foster the right environment for stewardship. This takes culture back to the roots we discussed earlier. You're not creating culture so much as cultivating it.

In other words, you're facilitating an ongoing conversation. Culture is at its highest level of impact when it's a living, evolving thing—a work-in-progress. Of course this comes with the challenges we've discussed, but we've also discussed both general and specific ways to craft it.

That conversation is going to be different depending on what stage of development your organization is at. If you're an early-stage company, then your task is to create and codify the emerging trust and values of the company, and also to lay out an initial vision. Once you've gone through your growing pains, the objective is to sustain the culture: to normalize and spread the behaviors and norms that define the company, and to guard against bad habits and complacency. In other cases, an established company loses its way and needs to renew its commitment to its culture, or it's out of step with the times and needs to reinvent itself through its culture.

Whatever the scenario, evolved leaders who lead through stewardship rather than rank, edict, and authority will first and foremost strive to embody the trust, values, and core behaviors that feed and nourish a healthy culture. And they will facilitate the conversation around culture just as they would any inclusive conversation—ensuring that everyone has a voice in the process, a seat at the table.

Leaders are not just facilitators, though. They're called leaders because they lead. They do things. They walk the walk. But when it comes to culture, that leadership is most effective when it focuses on laying out broad first principles as a foundation—and then facilitating a participatory process to flesh out those principles. The U.S. Constitution has been so successful because it avoids micromanaging or getting into the weeds. It establishes first principles and then gives the national culture room and air to breathe and evolve. The same approach works for company culture as well.

As in all conversations, there may be strong voices and positions, but there should be a dialogue where each person is invited to share, and others listen with hearts and minds. Too often, the top-down approach of thinking that culture comes from only senior leadership reinforces a monologue, and deference to the status quo and current power structure. It's perfectly acceptable to rigorously challenge an idea without attacking the person. Our discourse as a nation seems to struggle with this technique. Learning how to delicately frame candid discussions might be a tactical skill your teams need to develop, especially if the trust factor is low. Word choice matters, and perhaps even more, follow-up behavior matters.

So be prepared to walk the walk after you've talked the talk. Leaders should always lead by setting the example. It's about responsibility, not privilege. That means you'll take arrows in the front and back.

Identify Connectors and Torchbearers

If culture is a conversation, who are the connectors in your organization? They may be the middle managers who bear the most responsibility for supervising employees daily. They may also be those employees who, regardless of formal status, have a kind of unofficial authority with their peers. I compare these nexuses to the character Red played by Morgan Freeman in *The Shawshank Redemption*. If you've seen the movie or read the book, you'll know how Red was the go-to for almost anything, and he always had his finger on the pulse of what was happening across the Shawshank prison.

Who are your Reds, and how can you empower them?

Identify your most important connectors and make it a priority to engage with them in conversations around culture, purpose, and shared values. Those one-on-one conversations will set the tone for the larger conversation around organizational culture. Treating them as co-creators for an evolving culture that is a work-in-progress makes it clear that everyone who shapes the culture and is responsible for safeguarding it and growing it. Your connectors naturally have the trust of others. By developing your own relationship with them, you will transitively develop social trust with others.

Culture is a flame. You need all the torchbearers you can muster to keep it alive and pass it on.

CHAPTER 7

Brick by Brick: Small But Critical Steps Toward Building a Strong Culture

Some organizations are in a permanent rehearsal mode. They discuss, plan, prepare for when they have budget, when the new management team is in place, when they decide on the merger, when we fill vacancies, when the reorg is done. This ends up creating a culture that has learned to wait, delay, postpone. It's never the right time. Their competence is waiting, preparing. The company is a theatrical green room, a sophisticated waiting room populated by highly paid players. Their name should be Not Yet Inc.

—Leandro Herrero

Among advanced chess players, there's a concept known as the quiet move. It's not the move that's going to win you the game or capture the opponent's queen. In fact, it's not going to win you anything at all. It doesn't promise an instant payoff or obvious strategic advantage, the business of tactical moves. No, a quiet move has other things in mind.

A quiet move is foundational. It's about setting the groundwork for a later tactical move. It's like laying down an invisible brick. You are indeed building something, but the immediate effect is not noticeable. Your opponent may wonder what you're up to, may even think you've wasted a move. But you know better.

Here's writer William Hartston talking about quiet moves in chess:

"The quiet moves are the most difficult. The flashy sacrifices and bold attacks that fill chess columns and magazines are a relatively easy part of technique compared with finding the right moves when there are no tactical solutions."[28]

You could make the same observation about organizational culture. Business columns and leadership books are filled with flashy moves that promise to shake up your company's culture and deliver measurable results, like higher employee engagement, lower turnover, and, of course, increased profits.

A lot of these moves are culture theater. Even when there are some solid ideas in the mix, culture gurus overpromise by injecting traditional business metrics into their discussions of culture. That is simply the wrong lens for looking at culture. Culture is best assessed through the small data that never

---

[28] Hartston, William. "Chess: a quiet move is better than a flashy sacrifice."

shows up on a spreadsheet. The only metric that really matters is asking yourself, "What will I tell my children?"

Just as the savvy chess player isn't looking for an immediate payoff to a quiet move, the wisest leaders will lay the groundwork for great culture with small foundational steps that will pay big dividends down the road.

So in this concluding chapter, I'm going to review the major takeaways from each chapter and suggest some first steps for those looking to instill culture in a young company, or reinvigorate a culture that's gone stale, or reinvent a culture that's gone off the rails. Then I'll suggest some concrete steps you can make in the right direction.

This is not a formula or a recipe. You will see no phrases like "six scientifically proven steps guaranteed to hack your company's culture" in these pages. There is no preordained sequence of moves. Trust your instincts. Start with the steps that resonate with you. At this point in your reading of the book, you likely have a gut sense of where your culture may be lacking. But don't live in your own head; make sure you involve others in the process of initiating change.

And let me be clear: I'm not dismissing the importance of strategy and tactics. A strong chess player needs a solid strategy, and so do you. I'm not dismissing numbers, either. The numbers have to add up at some point. And certain metrics can be valuable signposts to tell you if your business is on the right track. What I am suggesting is that you not view culture through these lenses. Culture is its own thing. A living thing. Cultivating culture is more like tending a garden than building a machine.

1. What Is Culture?

- Culture is the invisible glue that holds a group together. It allows the group to become more than the sum of its parts.

- That glue starts with trust, with the social norms and unwritten rules that foster belonging and inclusion.

- Culture also involves a shared purpose by which members transcend individual self-interest and achieve something more than they could on their own.

- Culture is behavior. It lives in the small things we do repeatedly, especially in our interactions with others: how we demonstrate respect, how we show we value others (not just as fellow workers, but as whole human beings).

- Culture also lives in the big picture: in a North Star that inspires awe, keeping us humble and connected to something larger than ourselves.

Start Here

Try to capture in words that invisible glue holding your organization together. What in your organization inspires awe, humility, meaning, and shared purpose? It could be something from your mission statement. But if nothing there lights a fire inside, start from scratch. Any line of business can reach for awe. Remember Michelin's "Because so much is riding on your tires." Remember the hospital custodians who thought of themselves as healers. Find your version of Apple's "Think Different" campaign.

A simple formula about seeding culture to try out: These are the 3 non-negotiables here. 1) When A happens, we always do B and never C 2) We will always do N, no matter what 3) X will always be rewarded, never Y

2. How Do You Seed Culture?

- The trust that seeds great culture is created by social cues that communicate psychological safety: the gut sense we have of whether a group is a safe place for us to be ourselves.

- Leaders can go a long way toward fostering that sense of trust by being vulnerable and unapologetically their authentic selves. If leaders can't safely be vulnerable, then neither can others.

- The social cues that communicate safety are demonstrated through how we interact with others, but also in how we design shared spaces (physical and virtual)—the visuals, colors, and iconography of those spaces.

- Culture is about behavior. *Repeated* behavior. Not about pronouncements or the trappings of "culture theater."

- You cannot institutionalize culture through policy and procedure. Companies that attempt to do so (the Professional Model) are less resilient than those placing a premium on human connection (the Commitment Model).

Start Here

How well do you demonstrate and model vulnerability? How often do you use phrases like "I don't know," "I need your help," "What do you think?" or "I screwed up"? Make a point of demonstrating vulnerability and observe how doing so frees others to be more themselves. Share personal stories of failure, trial, and perseverance as invitations to open up conversation. Then as leader begin the process of letting go. The more you let go, the more control you actually have. If you think you can't, then the problem is you.

3. How Do You Sustain Culture?

- In its startup phase, a company is often fueled by the charisma, vision, and sheer will of its founder. Its culture is implicit and may seem to arise organically. As a company grows, the challenge is how to make culture explicit and pass it on to newcomers while empowering them to contribute their own verse.

- Although culture must be passed on to others, "onboarding" as typically practiced tends to be sterile, a one-way monologue coming from HR. Welcoming someone new into your organization should be a moment of high energy and curiosity. Find some awe in these moments. New talent brings new oxygen into your culture.

- Sustainable culture is all about feeding intrinsic motivation: that which we do because we find it inherently rewarding. Unlike forms of extrinsic motivation—like performance and profit—intrinsic motivation cannot be measured. A central intrinsic motivation for leadership should be to make your company a fulfilling place to work.

- When we are guided strictly by traditional performance metrics, we fall into the mindset of the Finite

Game—a view of business as a zero-sum game, one that values stability and predictability and shies away from surprise and risk. This mindset leads to calculations driven by self-interest, lack of foresight, and decisions to pump a subsequent quarter's metrics.

- Those metrics have their place, but your culture should be driven by a long-run or an Infinite Game mindset. This embraces the unfamiliar and the unknown and is comfortable in the absence of a clear finish line. This mindset strives for win-win solutions and nurtures a culture of trust, risk-taking, and innovation. This means not punishing employees who make mistakes as part of learning and discovery.

- While culture must be made explicit as your organization grows so you can pass it on to others, that explicit, codified part of the culture is just the tip of the iceberg. The depth of your culture, the part of the iceberg that sits below the water line, is all about the tacit, the implied, the unsaid.

Start Here

Challenge yourself and others to distill your own organizational culture in three short phrases. Try not to exceed ten words total. Avoid abstract corporate-speak words like "synergy" and "leverage." Think of rules or norms that guide, but that also create possibility rather than constrict. Your goal is to capture in words the tip of the iceberg while suggesting and creating space for everything below the surface. Involve a diverse group in this process and codify core principles. Establish expectations that culture is alive and will change.

The best organizational initiative around culture is one that doesn't exist because it's not needed. Think about what an organization that doesn't need one would look like and shape towards that if you can.

4. How Do You Scale Culture?

- As your organization grows in personnel and diversity and also expands across geography, you have some tough calls to make in terms of how decision-making and authority will flow. There is no one right answer. Looser structures are easier to pull off in some industries than others. Just know that, as you scale, structure has repercussions for your culture because of the attenuation of messaging across an org chart.

- Flat structures, less hierarchy, and self-managed teams encourage a more inclusive culture. Just as a physical space shapes the conversations that take place within it, your organization's structure will shape how employees talk and relate to one another.

- If you do choose a more traditional hierarchical structure as you grow and scale up, the quality of your managers—and of their own work experience—will contribute to the creation of a more engaged employee experience. Look for managers with a gift and calling for developing potential in others. Empower managers to be culture ambassadors instead of watchmen, list makers, and score keepers of who is naughty and nice.

- Some companies will scale up not just in size, but over distance. When you have a distributed or remote workforce, you need tools to foster the kind of connectivity that organically takes place around a water cooler. We've learned a difficult but important lesson through COVID-19 that rolling out videoconference programs don't equate to creating, fostering, and sustaining culture. Human connection needs more.

- As companies grow, they typically hire for cultural fit as a way of ensuring the founding culture will remain intact. But hiring for adaptability, empathy, creativity, and risk-taking may be a better route. Employees who can read social cues and adapt accordingly, who are flexible in the give-and-take of an evolving culture, thrive more in the long run than those who are a perfect fit but lack adaptability.

- When an organization grows, systems and process grow. As the systems become more complex, there is a point where managing the complexity of the system becomes a greater problem than managing the complexity of the external environment. All energy goes to managing the beast. Complexity begets complexity and human connection is lost.

- The ultimate goal in scaling culture is resilience: creating an environment that, even as the workforce expands, allows employees to be "in the flow zone." The flow zone is an optimal state that provides challenge but isn't out of reach. An organization in the flow zone will adapt quickly and respond to disruptions. A culture of resilience is safe, but the team members embrace risk and change. They creatively express themselves through solutions that delight customers.

Start Here

You want employees who can read social cues and adapt to your culture. But that adaptability should be a two-way street. Is management invested in cultivating employees and team members? Is there time for managers to do this, or is something they only do once a quarter? Are you reading your employees and adapting to their needs? Above and beyond preparing them for the tasks required for the job, do you have a larger vision of how to develop employees personally and professionally? If you chart the narrative of your customer journey, do the same for your employees. Your goal isn't to create a carnival every day, but instead, to develop a fulfilling workplace that is achievable with consistent effort, practice, and time. Challenge each other to consider what you want to create. What do you want to be proud of?

5. How Do You Change Culture?

- Many companies at a certain point come to a culture crossroads. You got complacent, and your culture grew stale. You're being challenged by young upstarts and need to retool and reinvent. Or a crisis has upended the entire economy (imagine that!) and everyone is trying to chart an uncertain new normal.
- The question is: can a tiger change its stripes? More often than not, no. Only 30% of organizational change programs succeed.
- One reason is *active inertia*: a tendency to protect the status quo, to revert to business as usual, to talk change but essentially stay within a well-worn groove. HR departments—in many cases, the ones charged with stewardship over a company's culture—are often the

biggest culprits here. They are miscast in their role.
Employee benefits don't represent culture.

- Other failed paths to change include trying to spin off a
cultural rebel from an established company—which is
what GM did with its defunct Saturn brand. This only
works when the spin-off has an organic connection
with the rest of the company, and when leadership
is committed to using it as a culture laboratory to
cultivate company-wide change. Spin-offs have
potential to create a new culture, but they can also
be in discord with the parent company. Acquisition
is another path, but heavy friction can emerge, and
cultures can feel like an arranged marriage.

- Mimicry is yet another common fail, as was the
case with United Airlines's TED division, a poorly
conceived attempt to mimic Southwest. Without an
authentic commitment to change, a facelift is not
going to fool anyone.

- So what *does* work? Among companies that have
successfully retooled their culture, a common denom-
inator stands out: addition by subtraction. Netflix
is one of a number of companies that reinvigorated
its culture by stripping away policies and rules and
procedures—and replaced bureaucracy and control
with meaningful freedom and autonomy.

Start Here

*What can you strip away in your own organization? What rules,
procedures, and levels of bureaucracy might be clogging the arteries*

of your culture? What would happen if you gave teams the power to self-manage and set their own budgets? What if employees could take time off whenever they felt they needed it? What if you gave people the freedom to work when and where and for how long they deemed necessary? This isn't a Six Sigma exercise to find some percent of increase efficiency. Humans are not robots in a factory. This is about how can you help facilitate and empower deeper human connection.

6. Who Owns Culture?

- Strip away unnecessary control and bureaucratic red tape, and culture (and people) thrive. The reverse is true as well. Behind most culture fails is excessive control, an overreliance on rules and procedures. And behind excessive control is a lack of trust. We started this book with the premise that culture begins with trust. If you don't trust your employees, why did you hire them in the first place? If your actual policies don't demonstrate that trust, your organization can never truly thrive because it will be built on a foundation of fear. Fear-based organizations require surveillance, and that is deadweight overhead your organization must bear.

- Hand-in-hand with a control mindset is a top-down view of culture: an assumption that culture is created in the C-suite and trickles down to the masses. Trickle-down economics didn't work, and neither does trickle-down culture. Culture is demonstrated at the top, but it also emerges from the ranks. It must meet in the middle and involve insights from all levels.

- The opposite mindset views culture as a conversation, one that includes everyone in the organization. If culture is the air that you breathe in the workplace, then it belongs to everyone. And if it belongs to everyone, the task of leadership is to facilitate that conversation—to be stewards of the culture, rather than keepers of it.

- When everyone owns the culture, they become stewards. If they have a voice and a stake in it, then your workplace is far more likely to provide employees with what self-determination theory posits are the three universal human needs: the need for connection, for autonomy, and for mastery. A thriving culture is inseparable from these needs.

- A top-down view of culture usually operates under the assumption that culture is a single, monolithic entity. Most organizations have distinct subcultures—a diversity that should be a strength. When everyone owns the culture, those subcultures are free to coexist as co-equals.

- Ownership may be a flawed way of looking at culture. Rather, reconsider "owners" as stewards, ambassadors, and emissaries, if employees can't actually own a piece of the company through stock. Ownership does offer a unique extrinsic motivation that triggers intrinsic feelings of value.

Start Here:

If culture is a conversation, who are the connectors in your organization? The informal leaders who set the tone for others? Identify your most important connectors and make it a priority to connect with them. Engage them in conversations around culture, and purpose, and shared values. Those one-on-one conversations will set the tone for the larger conversation around organizational culture. Don't pull people into an office to discuss culture, at least not right away. Power dynamics can affect that conversation. Start slowly because management's sudden and zealous interest can undermine trust. Remember that trust is earned in drops but lost in buckets.

Epilogue

At the time of my writing this epilogue, Americans are working out how, exactly, they're going to reopen their businesses. And in the conversation, it seems there's a reactionary desire to return to the past—as if the past were working perfectly well.

It certainly did for some. But COVID-19 laid bare weaknesses and flaws. They exist in our companies, our societal infrastructure, our health systems, our government, and our racial and political disparities.

Listening to people describe the effects of COVID-19 as surreal and unreal shows our disconnect with just how real it is, how critically important the need is to make drastic shifts in the way we live, do business, manage businesses, and conduct our society. The pandemic has exposed in sobering light what is valued and who is valued in our society. No question, our health care workers are essential . . . at least say think so. But then why the foot-dragging to get them the proper resources they need to do their job with maximum safety and efficiency? And beyond health care workers, how about the people bagging groceries, picking up our trash, delivering mail, and harvesting food? We now all see how essential they truly are. But will that recognition last? And what will it take for our culture to change?

I think that many seek a return to normal because there is the natural fear of not having our basic needs met. For some during COVID-19, they even came face-to-face with the fear of their mortality. Stay on this concept of *normal* for a moment. There is a scientific argument that normal is not . . . normal. Plagues are only in history books, but pathogens evolve regardless. With respect to our climate, we've experienced a relatively benign epoch between ice ages. From a geologic perspective, we experience the occasional earthquake, tsunami, or volcanic eruption. These take a major toll on lives and communities, but our Earth is a safe harbor compared to what we understand of its geologic past. On a galactic scale, we haven't been hit with the doomsday meteor in a while or a catastrophic gamma ray burst from a distant quasar. These events seem like Hollywood fiction, but they *can* happen. They are normal parts of existence. They aren't surreal. They are real.

With our 21st century perspective, we are used to normal. And that might be part of the issue. Normal seems to make us less resilient because it distances us from the world. Psychologically seeing the world through screens creates a derealization disorder. Everything seems like an episode of *Black Mirror*. Normal makes us complacent, a little too comfortable. We see now with the protests that returning to early 2020 isn't what's being demanded. People are willing to face a viral pandemic that can kill you to confront a pandemic of racial injustice. Being uncomfortable will push us to change and finally face the racial injustice that undermines our democracy and our culture.

I'm realistic and a jaded Gen Xer. I know that change won't happen in some great altruistic coming together for the sake of what is best for all. Unfortunately, change in our society is like someone only changing their poor health habits after being told they have heart disease and will be dead in a year if they continue their path. Many organizations in this time will push hard to return to their old ways. Many will spin a stylized new normal—which sounds like a cheap veneer on the old normal. Moving ahead with sincere change in our culture isn't just about figuring out how to create six feet of social distance between cubicle desks, our communal fridge, and the kombucha tap. Our culture in organizations isn't calling out for a mere physical design change, process reengineering, or a new employee handbook. Those things might be necessary, but they aren't sufficient to achieve organizational cultures of resilience. Again, normal wasn't working for large portions of society. So why do we just want an incremental 2.0 version of it? Likely, 2.0 would be a version defined *for* us, instead of by us.

Future-state thinking is what can help pull us forward. So much of inclusive, creative and innovative culture is about creating a shared mission around possibility and delivering on potential—both inside and outside of our organizations. We can't expect to create organizations where people thrive and then not carry out those values into other aspects of our lives. Otherwise, we're just lying to each other.

Change is upon the world. It always was. We experience it personally and in how we earn our livings. As individuals and organizations, we can anchor down to fight the future by holding onto the past. We can claw to get back to a normal. Yet holding back change is exhausting, and we all lose in the long run.

What about the other extreme, where we actively seek out change, risk, disruption, reinvention? Should we be in state of seeking and embracing tectonic shifts, or would that put us in an exhausting state of hypervigilance? It's not that farfetched because we all know of people like that, and many of us could even name companies that push the boundaries. Take SpaceX as one grand example, or the proliferation of local food trucks as a different example. The multitude of startups launching over the past twenty years shows that having an appetite for risk-taking is growing. Many people would prefer to bet on their own skills and resources rather than have their intellectual property pumped from them for a company that might never use or acknowledge their contribution. Startups have no choice but to be in a search mode, and founders ride the white lightning of risk all the time. I know this personally from my own experience as a founder of multiple companies. Maybe the time is nigh for tossing the ideal of normal. It's time for substantive change across all our companies, organizations, and institutions. Some would probably call that a revolution. It probably is because the evolution is too slow.

"Hard times create strong men. Strong men create good times. Good times create weak men. And weak men create hard times."

I agree with parts of that quote. But not the fatalistic and unbreakable wheel. COVID-19's impact on our lives and our businesses can be seen as an opportunity—not as in being opportunistic to capitalize on vulnerabilities, weakness, and pain—rather, it has accelerated and revealed too much truth to deny any longer. If an organization was looking for a reason (or an excuse) to change, if they need cover, this time in history is as good as any, I suppose. Looking at how quickly our society crashed and what has sustained us during lockdown, we have seen that the issues of connection, leadership, management, and workplace motivation are as relevant as ever.

Any worker who has spent a length of time on videoconferencing has experienced its failure to drive connection because it's a transactional tool, a glass wall between people. Other modalities are needed to create human connection. There is an exhausting feeling of isolation in our safer-at-home remote way of working. Conversely, we've also demonstrated we don't need to be a part of management's surveillance tactics, which have been the norm across so many organizations for decades. The safer-at-home workers have pushed on and accomplished much more without performance management, stay interviews, employee metrics, and soul-sucking touch bases. Those working and educating children at home also demonstrated a deeper source for engagement that arose from within themselves versus mandates from higher up on an org chart. We've now seen the attenuating usefulness in the established power hierarchy as defined in org charts and traditional ways of organizing. Working remotely has unmasked what leaders should actually be doing to fill people up in a time of fear and uncertainty. In the vacuum of competent leadership, workers demonstrate that if we take off the shackles of hierarchy, policy, procedure, and 1950s mechanized management, people are mission driven and strive to make a difference. Every day we have people working. We have people teaching. We have people helping. We have people marching. No rule book needed. How much more could they accomplish if their managers were thoughtful leaders who cleared the way for them?

So many people have been let down during this time. We've been let down as citizens, we've been let down as employees, we've been let down as taxpayers, we've been let down as loyal consumers of all the stuff shoveled our way. Where we see beacons of hope are in the small gestures between person to person and neighbor to neighbor. It's actually within the end-of-news broadcast human interest stories where the small seeds of possibility are being planted.

With that thought, we come full circle. Because all the training, education, books, webinars, seminars, keynotes, and consultants that I've listened to about organizational change make change seem overly complex. In part because it serves some to make it so. There are so many models. So many approaches. So many philosophies. Most of which just prepares us for the past.

Where to begin? The human-interest stories about organizations are where the cultural change begins. It's about establishing trust, connection, and relationships around a greater mission. Without trust, you will not have effective managers and no inspiring leaders. There will be no engagement. No performance. You will meet neither goals nor other metrics. There will be no point in returning to normal.

Begin.

Afterword

Storytelling—in particular, sharing origin stories—is a powerful, authentic tool that leaders can use to create trust and inspire team members to be great. Origin stories tend to inspire employees because they show that presidents and C-levels are human and flawed, too. My co-founder shared his story with me, and now I would like to pass it along to you.

An Origin Story About Trust, Connection, and Leadership

My maternal grandfather, Bernard "Ben" Precourt, was born in 1898. He grew up when airplanes were just taking flight, before the "Great War"—the name it was given before world wars needed a numbering system. He was from a family of potato farmers in Central Wisconsin's sand belt, and married my grandmother, Blanche, from northern Minnesota's iron range.

They had eight children over twenty-one years, Mom being the eighth and final one, born during the Second World War, but they raised most of the others through the Great Depression. In the 1930s, Ben was part of a team that brought rotary telephone systems from the East Coast to the Midwest; he helped implement the system and train others to use this groundbreaking technology. By the end of his career he had served as a driver of the AAA's motorist training program and also the school safety crossing guard programs, both of which led to enduring such services that still exist today. Meanwhile, Blanche served as the household CEO, as it is called in the 21st century. The family cemented their core values during those times—being wise with finances, trusting one another, and communicating well.

Mom's eldest siblings had children soon after she was born, so Mom became an aunt when she was still a just a baby. Ultimately, the eight children of Ben and Blanche had nearly three dozen children of their own. The relationships that resulted from this broad family, cemented by the experiences of a booming America in the 1940s, 50s, and 60s, led to a cohesive family structure that has endured well into the 21st century.

Ben passed on his ninetieth birthday, and at the event of the celebration of his life, Mom handed me his wedding band. She knew that my early years with my grandfather were critical to whom I had become—he showed the young me what it was like to live those experiences that formed him in the 1930s. He walked me back and forth to nursery school, he took me to buy eggs from a local farmer, and together we negotiated banana prices with the local grocery. ("I'll take those overripe bananas off your hands for five cents a pound," he'd say.) By giving me that ring, Mom was telling me to embody the best characteristics of the man that she looked up to more than any other, and I was honored.

I started wearing that ring on my right hand ring finger that day, and have done so every day since. It's a reminder of those core values, the wisdom of living wisely but simply, to show respect toward others, to teach and to inform, and to trust and empower.

When I got to the seventh grade, the class was put through the exercise of choosing a future career option. We were tasked with researching an education path and future salary potential for a particular career. Having seen my brother deal with eyeglasses since I was in the first grade, and having just been diagnosed with early myopia myself, I focused my research on optometry. The eye doctor changed my world when I picked up my first glasses—life for me was reinvigorated as trees again had detailed branches and leaves, and the bricks on houses had definition down to their sandy, granular surfaces. I wanted to help people like he had helped me.

I became a Doctor of Optometry and started a clinic as a solo practitioner, then became part of a partnership across multiple clinic locations. I found it easy to inspire and empower those who worked with me, and developed connections and created collaborative work models that led to trust and enduring relationships. This part of my work life was just as important as the patient care itself.

About ten years into practice, I was appointed to a national committee of eye doctors who were focused on improving the visual welfare of children, specifically infants. To complement the basic services already provided by pediatricians, our group aimed to have thousands of eye doctors offer a no-cost eye evaluation to infants in their first year of life, and over the course of five years we were successful in seeing this initiative become an engrained part of the profession. In that time, we worked as a cohesive team, despite being separated geographically across the entire nation, powered by the emerging technologies of the day: email and intranet boards.

The next step of my professional life was oddly amazing. Odd because I became a co-founder and CEO of a software company, a business that was entirely unknown to me when I started the endeavor. And amazing because this step of my work life changed my personal life for the better in every way. Our business was born and evolved significantly from our early days in the mid-2000s. From a technology perspective, this was a critical time when iPods were giving way to iPhones, and eventually, the public was being convinced it needed a tablet computing device called the iPad. This was when people could download music from the internet, followed by the ability to access their music on the internet... . "in the cloud." My co-founder was a technology expert who had worked in software development before the cloud was a thing, and he was building our system to be accessible on any computer through any internet browser—no downloads, no installs, no discs . . . just get online.

Once my co-founders and first employees had defined and built the early version of our system, we gained early customers, and we were making a disruptive impact in our market with our innovative software. But none of us were working in an office. We were entirely remote, a virtual workforce all working from home offices. The technology of the day was Skype, originally built for international telephony, but which carried the ability to instant message and speak through audio connections. It even allowed video interactions, and the first five of us met regularly in a way that allowed us to build and advance our relationships better than the traditional phone conference.

By the time we grew to a couple dozen employees, we had outgrown Skype. Still entirely remote, our team was doing great things for our customers through our product, but it was increasingly difficult to stay connected as a team. We leveraged Skype as best we could, but it was frankly incapable of allowing us to maintain a cohesive work relationship. So we tried an intranet and some other systems to allow other touchpoints. Nothing worked to share consciousness and develop trusting relationships.

Then one day an eye care patient came into my clinic, and I found the next "co-founder" in my life. Scott Kohl was an experienced business leader with a background in gaming companies. His company was building gamified solutions to help businesses create new levels of connectedness with their customers. We started an ongoing dialogue about how a team of virtual employees might benefit from a technology system that we would build together, one that would embody connectedness and collaboration, and from which would result a sense of trust and common purpose.

The business started as an idea for a virtual water cooler, harking back to the days when people in a company would cross paths while stepping away from their desks and chat about anything from a work project to a basketball game to a dance recital. A software product was built that created opportunities for asynchronous conversations instead of actual trips to the water cooler, and then in 2018 it was officially positioned as ThirdSpace.

The first space is your personal life, and the second space is your work life. Instead of aiming on work-life separation or balance, the third space is where the two intersect. Literal third spaces are actual places like coffee shops, libraries, break rooms, cafeterias, or parks, all of which allow their visitors to do work, to do life, and to enjoy the intersection of both. ThirdSpace aims to be the software-powered, virtual expression of those actual places.

Today, ThirdSpace aims to help a business by connecting every employee into an enterprise social and work network, with the goal of driving connectedness and collaboration, resulting in a trusting environment that optimizes employee satisfaction, retention, and performance because they are invited by their employer to bring their whole self to the work experience. It allows for epic culture to result from groups of people who are socially distant but emotionally connected.

Working to build this company has been the expression of a lifetime of experiences of connectedness. My goal of connecting with my co-workers is an expression of everything I ever wanted for my clinic teams and then later my software teams. The utilization of technologies has always been at the core of the functional solution. And those technologies we use today are extensions of the rotary phones that my grandfather planted into our lives, nearly one hundred years ago.

I still have the ring on my right hand, continuously reminding me of Ben Precourt, of the family that he and Blanche created, of the connections and the trust and love that resulted. Through various business experiences, those core values have never left me. I'm thrilled that each journey has resulted in something that has allowed me to better collaborate with those who have joined me on the journey to success.

Dr. Scott Jens

References

Accenture. "Getting to Equal: The Hidden Value of Culture Makers." 2020. https://www.accenture.com/_acnmedia/ Thought-Leadership-Assets/PDF-2/Accenture-Getting-To-Equal-2020-Research-Report.pdf.

Coyle, Daniel. *The Culture Code: The Secrets of Highly Successful Groups.* New York: Bantam Books, 2018.

Csikszentmihaly, Mihaly. *Flow: The Psychology of Optimal Experience.* New York: Harper Perennial Modern Classics, 2008.

Duhigg, Charles. "What Google Learned from Its Quest to Build the Perfect Team." *The New York Times Magazine,* February 25, 2016. https://www.nytimes.com/2016/02/28/magazine/ what-google-learned-from-its-quest-to-build-the-perfect-team. html.

Dvorak, Kate and Pendell, Ryan. "Want to Change Your Culture? Listen to Your Best People." March 6, 2019. https://www.gallup. com/workplace/247361/change-culture-listen-best-people. aspx.

Edmondson, Amy. "Psychological Safety and Learning Behavior in Work Teams." *Administrative Science Quarterly* 44, no. 1 (1999): 350-83. doi:10.2307/2666999.

Glazer, Emily and Rexrode, Christina. "Wells Fargo CEO Defends Culture, Lays Blame with Bad Employees." *The Wall Street Journal,* September 13, 2016. https://www.wsj.com/articles/ wells-fargo-ceo-defends-bank-culture-lays-blame-with-bad-employees-1473784452.

Hamel, Guy. "First Let's Fire all the Managers." *Harvard Business Review.* December 2011. https://hbr.org/2011/12/first-lets-fire-all-the-managers.

Harter, Jim. "How Coronavirus Will Change the 'Next Normal' Workplace." May 1, 2020. https://www.gallup.com/workplace/309620/coronavirus-change-next-normal-workplace.aspx.

Hartston, William. "Chess: a quiet move is better than a flashy sacrifice." *The Independent,* July 20, 1993. https://www.independent.co.uk/arts-entertainment/chess-a-quiet-move-is-better-than-a-flashy-sacrifice-1485965.html.

Hickman, Adam and Robison, Jennifer. "Is Working Remotely Effective?" January 24, 2020. https://www.gallup.com/workplace/283985/working-remotely-effective-gallup-research-says-yes.aspx#.

Kanter, Rosabeth Moss. "Transforming Giants." *Harvard Business Review.* February 2008. https://hbr.org/2008/01/transforming-giants.

Kellaway, Lucy. "Hands up if you can say what your company's values are." *Financial Times,* October 4, 2015. https://www.ft.com/content/d508d08e-682d-11e5-a57f-21b88f7d973f.

Kwak, Mary. "Commitment Counts." *Sloan Review.* July 15, 2001. https://sloanreview.mit.edu/article/entrepreneurship-commitment-counts/.

Lehrer, Jonah. "The Paradox of Altruism." February 28, 2012. https://www.wired.com/2012/02/the-paradox-of-altruism.

Lyons, Rich. "Three Reasons Why Culture Efforts Fail." *Forbes.com.* September 27, 2017. https://www.forbes.com/sites/richlyons/2017/09/27/three-reasons-why-culture-efforts-fail/#690d72a0e077.

Mance, Henry. "The Rise and Fall of the Office." *Financial Times.* May 15, 2020. https://www.ft.com/content/f43b8212-950a-11ea-af4b-499244625ac4.

McCord, Patty. "How Netflix Reinvented HR." *Harvard Business Review*. January 2014. https://hbr.org/2014/01/how-netflix-reinvented-hr.

Nickisch, Curt, host. "Creating Psychological Safety in the Workplace." *HBR IdeaCast* (podcast). January 22, 2019. https://hbr.org/podcast/2019/01/creating-psychological-safety-in-the-workplace.

Parker, Clifton. "Stanford research shows that working together boosts motivation." *Stanford News*. September 15, 2014. https://news.stanford.edu/news/2014/september/motivation-walton-carr-091514.html.

Pentland, Alex. "The New Science of Building Great Teams." *Harvard Business Review*. April 2012. https://hbr.org/2012/04/the-new-science-of-building-great-teams.

Semler, Ricardo. "Managing Without Managers." *Harvard Business Review*. September 1989. https://hbr.org/1989/09/managing-without-managers.

Sinek, Simon. *The Infinite Game*. New York: Portfolio, 2019.

Sull, Donald. "Why Good Companies Go Bad." *Harvard Business Review*. July 1999. https://hbr.org/1999/07/why-good-companies-go-bad.

Taleb, Nassim Nicholas. *Antifragile: Things That Gain from Disorder*. New York: Random House, 2012.

Walsh, Dylan. "Look Beyond 'Culture Fit' When Hiring." *Insights by Stanford Business*. February 2, 2018. https://www.gsb.stanford.edu/insights/look-beyond-culture-fit-when-hiring.

Wigert, Ben and Maese, Ellyn. "How Your Manager Experience Shapes Your Employee Experience." July 9, 2019. https://www.gallup.com/workplace/259469/manager-experience-shapes-employee-experience.aspx.

Zax, David. "Want to be Happier at Work? Learn How from These Job Crafters." *Fast Company*. June 3, 2013. https://www.fastcompany.com/3011081/want-to-be-happier-at-work-learn-how-from-these-job-crafters.